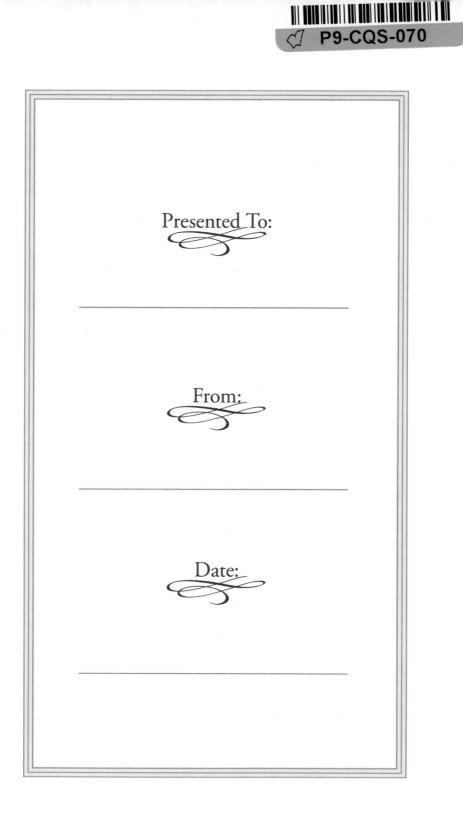

Presented To:

_____

From:

_____

Date:

_____

HEARING
AND UNDERSTANDING
THE VOICE OF
GOD

HEARING
AND UNDERSTANDING
THE VOICE OF
GOD

FRANK A. DECENSO, JR.

DESTINY IMAGE® PUBLISHERS, INC.

P.O. Box 310, Shippensburg, PA 17257-0310

"Speaking to the Purposes of God for this Generation and for the Generations to Come."

This book and all other Destiny Image, Revival Press, MercyPlace, Fresh Bread, Destiny Image Fiction, and Treasure House books are available at Christian bookstores and distributors worldwide.

For a U.S. bookstore nearest you, call 1-800-722-6774.
For more information on foreign distributors, call 717-532-3040.
Or reach us on the Internet: www.destinyimage.com.

Trade Paper ISBN 13: 978-0-7684-3803-1
Ebook ISBN 13: 978-0-7684-8988-0

For Worldwide Distribution, Printed in the U.S.A.
1 2 3 4 5 6 7 8 9 10 11 / 16 15 14 13 12 11

CONTENTS

FOREWORD

HEARING AND UNDERSTANDING THE VOICE OF GOD

by Christy Wimber

Hearing God's voice is vital to us as believers. What is God's desire for our lives, within our homes and families, as well as for our churches? We are constantly bombarded with so much noise that the ability to hear and see what God's up to can often be a struggle. Sometimes it feels impossible to hear His voice with so much distraction. In fact, many times it can be downright frustrating to hear and understand what God is saying about our lives. No matter the distractions, God shares what He is doing or about to do with those who take the time to have knowledge of the One who holds all the answers. To know Him is to know His voice. For the most part, every believer wants to know God's will for their lives, but their discipline must match their desire. If you want to know God's will for your life, you must also be willing to invest in the disciplines that give us such clarity.

If you want to have revelation, I believe you first must have intimacy. People often say to me that they want to know what God is saying, and they want to get revelation as to what He's up to. Yet, I have found, in my limited understanding, that most revelation is birthed out of intimacy.

And hearing God's voice is one thing; understanding it is completely different. Remember, it was Jesus who said, *"You will be ever hearing, but never understanding"* (Matt. 13:14 NIV). If we hear God, we must also understand the message. God speaks to us through various means so we can begin to understand who He is. But part of understanding what God is saying consists of hearing things through His heart and not our own. Our filter isn't clear enough. That's why we're called to have the mind of Christ, not the mind of us (see Phil. 2:5). We first must understand who He is, so when He speaks, we will know the purpose. God never speaks to us through just one person or one place but, more often than not, through many people and places. I believe it is necessary that we avoid becoming too nearsighted in the areas we live and serve; otherwise, we cannot hear the heart of God through others who hear him through different lenses.

Many different vessels use a variety of ways to reveal God's heart to us. Just think about the way God speaks to us through creation alone. David expressed this all throughout the Psalms, and worship often followed His realization of what God had done. All throughout creation, His beauty surrounds us and speaks loudly of who He is. Throughout the earth, all creation groans at the creativity of our Creator. He is the great Creator who is still creating.

The real question isn't, *Is God speaking?* The real question lies within our ability to hear His voice. Only when we hear and understand the voice of God will we be able to be on the front lines of what's about to break through in creativity. If we are His kids, then we should be the ones who are the most innovative—seeing and releasing those things that have never been seen, heard of, or released. Just think about our King as the great Creator. If we press into Him, we will catch His heart and hear His voice regarding what He wants to create next.

Look at the providence of God. Seeing how God cares for us shows us His heart. Remember, God said that He cares for the lilies, so how much more will He care for us (see Matt. 6:28-30)? He speaks His knowledge of care so loudly as He takes care of all the needs we have in life. His mercies are new every morning; He is our great provider, our Jehovah Jireh. His heart is revealed to us as He cares for all those things that we don't even know we're in great need of. He knows the comfort we will need, so in His great provision, He sends us the comfort of His Holy Spirit who is also our Counselor, the one who guides us through the journey. How can we be counseled unless we hear?

If we're going to understand what God is saying, we must know His words by His Word. Remember, the Bible is one of the many ways that God speaks truth to us, and truth is what sets and keeps us free (see John 8:32). These are the Words of Jesus Himself and they reveal both His conversations with our spiritual forefathers as well as with our Father in Heaven. The Word of God reveals time and again what it looks like to be dependant on the words of God. Just look at the various interactions between Jesus and the Father. These intimate conversations are what gave Jesus the ability to understand what the Father was up to.

Do you remember that Jesus could only do what the Father had shown Him? What if we did only those things God had spoken to us? Would your life look different if you were only doing things God Himself had initiated? The words the Father spoke to Jesus were the only way Jesus could accomplish what He set out to do. It is the same today: His still small voice hits us in the core of who we are, directing us in the same way the Father directed Jesus. Jesus Himself modeled hearing and understanding what the Father is saying so that we can change the course of history too.

It is vital we get in tune with what God is speaking. And because it's a relationship, it's a choice to learn to listen to how one speaks. I have two children, Camie Rose and John Richard II. They have been with me their whole lives. They sit with me, and we take the time to talk about what's going on and what decisions need to be made next. They have heard me tell them time and again how I care for them and how proud I am. It has been years of learning and understanding each other. They are both different in so many ways; yet, when we come together, we all meet because we value and love each other.

They are with me so much that I can be in the other room and yell out to them and they know it's my voice. Why? Because they know me, and I know them.

It's relationship. It's putting time and effort into the relationship we say that we value. Remember the power that Christ's words carry? They are Spirit and Life to us (see John 6). When we hear His words, they hit our spirit reminding us we belong to Him and giving us the life we need. His words impacted the disciples in the same way. Peter said to Jesus, "Where else can we go? You hold the very words of life" (see John 6:68). His voice brings everything important back into perspective. His words remind us that He matters most. His promise is that He will not withdraw or hold back, but that those who seek after Him will find Him. If we knock, He will open doors (see Matt. 7:7). His heart is not that we would be lost, but that we would be found.

I want to encourage you to take the time to listen. Discover how God speaks to you—Spirit to spirit, like He says in Romans where He calls out to us in our spirits, reminding us that we're His kids. You belong to Him. And my prayer is if you take the time to be with Him, nothing else will be as important. It will bring your life into clear perspective of who you are, and what you're made for.

And in your life, no matter the distractions, may His voice be the loudest.

CHRISTY WIMBER
Yorba Linda Vineyard
Senior Leader

1

DREAMS AND VISIONS OF DESTINY

by Barbie L. Breathitt

Before time began, before natural light existed or the worlds were formed, God had a dream. He spoke across a dark void of emptiness and brought order out of chaos. He brought direction to a vacuous expanse of nothingness. The all-powerful God hung the worlds on the might of His Word. He flung the constellations into space, suspending galaxies upon an invisible structure that continues to expand into the eons of eternity. This same all-knowing, creative, omnipresent God invades the small windows of our hearts each night through the realm of dreams. He takes the formless and void places in our lives and injects His heavenly spectrums of colored light to form images of hope and destiny. He embraces us with words of love that frame our lives and creates endless possibilities for us to explore. (See Genesis 1:3-5.)

Before Adam fell, he understood the mysteries of the universe because he communed with God. Everything God creates is full of His majestic light, power, and beautiful splendor. God's nature is love and He is light. Out of these united substances, God speaks creative words to release life and restoration and revelation into our dreams.

God reminded Job that He was present when Jesus created the universe.

> *Where is the way to the dwelling of light? And darkness, where is its place, that you may take it to its territory and that you may discern the paths to its home?* **You know, for you were born then, and the number of your days is great!** *(Job 38:19-21 NASB)*

God etched His promises on man's spirit as the foundations of the world were being formed. God shook Job out of his apathy and depression by restoring revelation, knowledge, and hidden mysteries.

> *Then the Lord answered Job out of the whirlwind and said, "Who is this that darkens counsel by words without knowledge? Now gird up your loins like a man, and I will ask you, and you instruct Me!* ***Where were you when I laid the foundation of the earth? Tell Me, if you have understanding, Who set its measurements? Since you know.*** *Or who stretched the line on it? On what were its bases sunk? Or who laid its cornerstone, when the*

*morning stars sang together and all the sons of God
shouted for joy?"* (Job 38:1-7 NASB)

Angels shouted as Jesus, the eternal Word, spoke laying the
cornerstone, writing His word upon the hearts of every person.
Our dreams cause us to remember who we are in God, the
chosen and called. We, like Job, were present in God the day
the universe was formed.

The building blocks that form a firm foundation for spiritual
growth reflect Jesus, the cornerstone. He gives us the insight we
need to recognize our divine connecters. He is our source of confidence. He empowers us to participate in His divine nature and
godliness. His power gives us everything we need to have a prosperous life including faith, goodness, knowledge, self-control,
perseverance, brotherly kindness, and love. These character traits
are all necessary for our spiritual growth. God-given dreams continually work on bringing clarity to immature areas in our lives.
Dreams have a transforming ability if we will respond to their
messages and directives.

God's creative promises caused something wonderful to
come out of nothing. The heavenly light of God's Word brings
insight and creative, color-saturated images into the dreamer's
spirit. When God breathes into our dreams, it sets His creative
transforming force into action. God's breath gives the spirit of
humankind knowledge, understanding, and life. It is by God's
grace that we obtain revelation knowledge of the invaluable
promises God grants us. These magnificent promises enable us
to become partakers of His divine nature. God's grace and peace
help bring understanding of the surpassing knowledge of the
mystery of Christ in us, the hope of glory.

Seeing that His divine power has granted to us everything pertaining to life and godliness, through the true knowledge of Him who called us by His own glory and excellence. For by these He has granted to us His precious and magnificent promises, so that by them you may become partakers of the divine nature (2 Peter 1:3-4 NASB).

Dreams empower us to see God's promises manifest. We can then believe what was previously only a fleeting thought. Dreams bring our imagination into the tangible realm of faith. We begin to believe what we see with the eyes of our spirit and with our natural eyes. In this sense, seeing is believing God Himself, who communicates through His Spirit to us through dreams.

God-given dreams carry a creative ability because they are prophetic in nature. God-given dreams come to change us into His image. God-given dreams enable us to walk in the Spirit with a renewed understanding of His vision, purpose, or plans for us. Dreams position us to embrace the promises of God. Dreams are just one of the many vehicles God has chosen to show and tell us who we are called to be in Christ. His desire is for us to reach our full potential and to be successful (see Ps. 24:1).

God-given dreams reveal keys to unlock the richness of life. The closer we come to the Lord, the more we see our need to resonate with the sounds of Heaven, to establish His Kingdom on earth. God has tuned each person like a unique instrument that releases a specific sound or new song in the orchestra of life. When we learn to walk as sons of God, in the fullness of unity (or harmony) with the sounds of the Kingdom of Heaven, earth will respond. God commands blessings upon us as we harmonize with the dreams He designs for our lives.

God has called us as mediators on the earth. We bring Heaven to earth through our dreams, decrees, prayers, prophecies, declarations, praise, and worship. God wants us to cry out to Him for wisdom and understanding. Just as He created the stars to light the heavens (see Ps. 147:4-5), God releases light and sound through dreams to cause His voice to resonate throughout creation.

Our dreams are a gateway for God to visit us. Through our dreams, God separates and dispels the darkness of sin and replaces it with the colors of His glorious light. He eliminates the chaos in our lives and brings us into perfect order to unlock our destiny by painting a brilliant new life story (see Prov. 3:5-6).

MIRROR IMAGE OF THE CREATOR

Dreams reflect the mirror image of the Creator as our minds are renewed by receiving and applying His Word. If our spirit is immersed in the living, transforming Word of God and is prayerfully developed in its fullness by consistent times of intimate communication with God, our spirit can receive grace to partake of His precious and magnificent promises obtainable through His divine power.

God communicates to the soul of man through dreams. As we meditate on God upon our beds, our souls begin to dialogue with God and He responds to us through dreams that dramatize our intimate conversation.

A dream aligns us with the present moment and reflects our true selves. If we will contemplate our dreams, we will see qualities of ourselves represented by characters or symbols in the dream. Because we are destined to reflect God's image as we come to know Him better, the closer we draw to God, the better we can reflect His love. His light reveals our condition as well as His unconditional love that changes us because we see ourselves clearly. We are Children of Light because our Creator is the Father of Lights. We are called to live a life where nothing is hidden from His sight, and everything is exposed to His light. Anything concealed in darkness will only distract us from our destiny and will eventually cause us to stumble and fall. Dreams bring God's brilliant enlightenment and love to our lives by dispelling darkness.

Dreams enable us to look past the present circumstances of our lives to see the endless possibilities that await our discovery in the eternal realm of the Spirit. The Kingdom of God is invisible because its vastness is without end. From this eternal realm come visions of the night, which spark faith and release hope for our present, near future, and all eternity.

God projects pictures upon the screens of our hearts. He speaks tenderly with life-giving creative words. If we will embrace these messages with faith and obedience, we will be transformed. If we ignore His dream messages, we will remain the same. Unchanged people forget who they are called to be and risk never reaching their destiny or fully maturing into the character of Christ.

DREAMS AND DESTINY

Dreams are at times a mirror image of the soul. They reflect our inner condition by revealing what will transpire if changes do not take place in us. Dreams are like relationships we maintain with friends. If we nurture them, they will grow and develop. If we ignore or neglect them, they will vaporize and disappear. If we honor our dreams, by writing them down and prayerfully following their instruction, they will become wise counselors to us. But if we ignore our dreams, they will not flourish.

God has programmed every person's spirit with the understanding of who He has made him or her to be. Our spirit knows who we are destined to be and the paths we must take to get there. Our part is to embrace God's plan through faith by cooperating with His changes and trusting Him to take obedient risks in life. To live according to who we really are, we must allow our life's dream to order our steps. God gives crucial directions through dreams, and it's important that we pay attention to them.

Having a greater measure of the Holy Spirit's guiding light also helps direct our lives. God's promises are the foundational laws of His Kingdom. Light-saturated revelation from God causes truth to invade our past, present, and future situations.

Many people are on a quest to discover the reason they exist and their God-given purpose in destiny. God's wisdom is often revealed in the mystery of a dream. The foremost question people ponder is, *What are my dreams trying to tell me about my destiny?* (see 1 Corinthians 2:7-9).

Understanding dreams requires that dreamers develop their spiritual gifts and skills. Our spiritual ears must be tuned to hear the Creator's voice as well as the voice of our own soul as it searches for God. More importantly, our spiritual eyes must also be focused to see into the realms of faith to behold and retain the fleeting images that play upon the screens of our mind's eye.

TRAINED THROUGH PRAYER

How do we develop our ability to understand a spiritual voice when we are so used to hearing the voices in the world dictate who we are and what we should be doing with our lives? There is a renewing of our minds and a changing of our hearts through love that must happen to allow our spirit man to take the lead. The Holy Spirit speaks the Word that gives us life and creates the vision to follow so we can fulfill our dreams and reject the dictates of the world.

How do we train our spiritual eyes to discern the unseen eternal realms that are featured every night in our dreams and visions? How do we sensitize our spirit to know when God has invaded our dreams? One avenue is by receiving His love through prayer.

Desperate prayer caused the Lord to remember Hannah and heal her barren life. The Lord gave her more than a son in Samuel. He gave her a prophet and a seer for a nation. The Lord stood before Samuel in the vision realm focusing Samuel's eyes to see. The God of all creation called Samuel's name audibly several times, tuning his ears to hear. Eli instructed Samuel to lie down and rest to wait for the coming of the Lord. Allow me to paraphrase what Eli said to Samuel, "Acknowledge the presence of the Lord when he comes, and declare you have ears to hear his voice" (author's paraphrase, see 1 Sam. 3:7-10).

The seer, the prophet, and the watchmen of God are coming into a new dream realm of vision and spiritual understanding. God is orchestrating divine encounters. He is pouring out dreams and visions in an increased measure upon all flesh (see Acts 2:17-18).

VISIONS SPEAK OF THE FUTURE

It is necessary to prepare our hearts to see our future and experience destiny in our own God encounters. God reveals the future in dreams so we can prayerfully bring the future into our present. Habakkuk 2:2 tells us to write down the visions God shows us so the message is clear, easy to read, and understandable. Visions speak of a future time that is appointed to come. We will obtain the vision if we believe it, prepare, and continue to patiently wait.

The ministry of the seer brings a major shift from just hearing the Word of God to *seeing* the plans of God unfold in dreams and visions. It is easier to remember a spectacular sight, because it imprints on our soul more than words that echo in our ears. We are visual beings; without a clear vision we remain naked, uncovered, and finally perish.

If we will lie down in peace to position ourselves in a place of covenant rest, God will visit us in our dreams. He may even appear to us nightly in the realms of the Spirit. We are always trying to be "human doings" when God has called us to be "human beings." God wants us to be at rest in His presence to hear His voice, experience His intimate love, and see a vision of who we are in the future (see 1 Sam. 3:11-14).

The Bible is full of God-given revelation through dreams, visions, and prophecy. We study to show ourselves approved so that we can operate in the Spirit of understanding and be spiritually fruitful (see 2 Tim. 2:15). We must learn from the Holy Spirit to discern between good and evil. Godly character will reject the evil and embrace the truth. In Ephesians 1:17-19, Paul prays that believers may be enlightened in our understanding in order to have the riches of God's glorious power manifest in our lives. This means that every believer must be led by the Holy Spirit's wisdom and revelation to understand the Father's heart.

The presence of God residing in our lives enables us to live the impossible dream. We do well to adopt the prayer of Moses in Exodus 33:13-16, when Moses asked God to show him His ways. This involves seeing the spiritual realm of vision. If we are able to see our future and understand the ways God wants us to walk, we will prosper. It is time to see the grace and favor of God resting upon us in the realms of glory. When our love for God and others is overflowing, it will demonstrate the reality of His glorious presence and the truth of the Gospel of the Kingdom.

WISDOM IN DREAMS

Dreams are like fleeting vapors. They appear for a brief moment in time and then vanish away forever if not captured. Dreams that are captured become a precious treasure from God. We need to ask God for dreams to obtain these elusive treasures and answers. Boldly seek God for revelatory significance that unfolds by receiving His dream messages. Continue to knock in order to acquire the interpretation and then simply believe. The mysteries God seals within our spirits create urgency within to seek after Him for the keys to unlock the treasures He has deposited (see Ps. 9:10).

God loves to use dreams to reawaken us with prophetic insight and to spur us forward toward our destiny in Him. To reach our full potential and God-given destiny, we must always set the Lord before us and stay focused on His plans. We must see ourselves as God sees us and interpret our dreams according to His loving nature,

His divine words, and His creative language to us, not according to what humanity says or even what we believe about ourselves.

Dreams are also given to direct us onto the proper paths in life. To discover these paths we must learn to read the sign posts and properly interpret the symbols on our dream maps. Interpreting dreams is more than being able to recall the dream's events. It is being able to discern the wisdom that our dreams contain and apply it accordingly.

Our relationship with God grows under the guidance of the Holy Spirit. As we ask him for discernment, wisdom, and understanding, the Lord will direct and guide our paths, often using dreams to teach us. Without the understanding of our dreams, we can remain in unfruitful darkness, but with understanding we can be saved, healed, and delivered (see Prov. 2:3-12).

God is the only one who knows the future. God has a divine dream plan for us to be successful and achieve our destiny in life. He reveals the paths of success in our dreams, so our hope remains in Him. Jeremiah 29:11 reveals the Father's heart to us. When our lives are diverted from God's planned path, He sends a dream to correct our course and restore hope in a prosperous future. As we pray for understanding and seek His wisdom with a sincere heart, we will find the answers to life's quest. God enables those who remain on His path to be strengthened (see Job 17:9).

Dreams bring us heavenly wisdom. Spiritual perceptions rain down upon open hearts to receive God's saving grace and knowledge (see Isa. 45:8). The dreams God sends speak the truth to us in love so we can grow up into Him. Christ holds the whole Body together and empowers each part to do its work.

In a society where success is expressed through accomplishments, financial stability, and busy schedules, God often talks to us the only way He can—when we are asleep. This may be the only time that we are quiet enough to hear Him. Dreams reveal our emotions, our pain, future events, and even hidden things of darkness. The puzzle pieces that God uses in dreams are part of His divine language. God gives us understanding as He searches the intents of our thoughts and hearts. If we seek God with our whole heart, we will find Him. While we sleep, our soul continually searches to make intimate contact with God. Dreams give us God's perspective to steer us away from harmful events and to give us life, vision, direction, provision, and a clear picture of our destiny.

A scoffer may seek wisdom and find none, but spiritual knowledge comes easily to one who has an understanding heart. Wisdom rests in the hearts of those who, like Solomon, seek to have spiritual understanding of their dreams.

A true dreamer is one who sees the impossible, and knows through God it will become possible. Dreamers are able to see the shadow of things to come as if by moonlight. By joining their faith to believe, the rays of the morning's dawn bring understanding and clarity (see Job 33:15-18).

Our dreams are God's answers to the hidden questions we conceal within. Once the reality of our dreams are embraced, we have the courage and fortitude to give them life and expression. As we bring our cares to God, He delivers us. The Word of the Lord is living and active. It penetrates the barriers of the soul, reaching our inner spirit to reveal the secrets in our hearts. We are laid bare and become transparent; nothing is hidden in its light.

ANGELS AND REALMS OF GLORY

Biblical history testifies that God has spoken to humankind through dreams since the beginning of time. Our dream life is like a highway on which messages are carried to the mind's eye and then to the spirit. These communications may come from a variety of sources: from the business of the day; from the body; from the soul; from the demonic realm; or from God and his angelic messengers.

Angels are heavenly messengers who are comprised of fire, wind, light, and the breath of God's Spirit. They appear in dreams and visions or come in visitations to deliver messages to guide us into God's pure truth.

Angels enter our dreams to bring messages from God's eternal realm. The Holy Spirit hovers over humankind, tenderly embracing us at night while favoring us with dreams that call us to pursue Him wholeheartedly.

God created the principle of becoming what we behold. Jacob grew exceedingly prosperous by seeing and hearing God's plan in a dream and by following the angel's instructions. Divine strategies are created from the dream fibers of moral excellence, character, integrity, and love.

We determine the amount and type of light that we are able to receive in dreams. The white light of God's kingdom draws the angelic realm to us so that we will shine with His light and draw others to His Kingdom. Angels are very active in our dreams—leading, guiding, and helping to direct us to the proper interpretations. The spiritual garments of light we wear are dependent upon the words we speak and the visions we believe. God is able to turn our darkness into His light (see Ps. 18:28).

God's light in our dreams will draw angels toward us. The Holy Spirit trains us to grow in spiritual discernment. He will open our eyes to see the glory realms of His majestic splendor, heavenly creatures, hosts of lights, and the angels. As we speak God's words of life, effectual doors of opportunity open. Words build a spiritual framework around us that form the atmosphere we exist in. We are responsible for creating a positive life by the choices we make and the words we pray and say every day (see Heb. 11:3).

By walking in God's divine nature, we are witnesses to the angelic realms. In John 11:40, *Jesus said to her, "Did I not say to you that if you would believe you would see the glory of God?"* (NKJV). Dreams reveal realms of glory. When we develop our ability to "believe" the things of God with our hearts, and not just our minds, we are able to walk in a spiritual understanding of the mysteries of days to come.

DANIEL AND JOSEPH— DREAM MINISTERS

Daniel was known as a man of great godly wisdom with an excellent spirit; knowledgeable, with great understanding, able to interpret dreams, solve riddles, and explain enigmas. Daniel's spiritual intimacy enabled the deep of God to reveal deep and hidden mysteries to the deep in Daniel. No secret troubled Daniel. He was even able to explain the handwriting on the wall (see Dan. 5:24-29). World rulers said of him, *"the Spirit of God is in you... light and understanding and excellent wisdom are found in you"* (Dan. 5:14 NKJV).

Joseph was severely tested by the Word of God until it finally perfected his character, releasing him from the shackles that bound him. Finally, he was propelled into his destiny in front of kings and rulers. (See Genesis 39-49.) Daniel and Joseph were able to accurately discern and reveal mysteries to all who came before them, great and small. Where are the gifted dream interpreters who are called to stand before the Pharaohs of our day?

Daniel saw that the wise will be enlightened to shine like stars, being able to ascend and descend an invisible heavenly ladder as they increase in the knowledge of God's ways (see Dan. 12:3-4). This verse speaks of man's natural knowledge as well as the increased knowledge and understanding of the mysterious ways of God. God-given dreams reveal spiritual truths that have been sealed (see Job 33:15-18). Daniel tapped into God's revelatory realm. He was shown futuristic insights and end-time revelation. Daniel was told to seal up these words until the time when knowledge of God's ways will increase and people will be purged and refined with fire (see Dan. 12:10). Daniel knew how to decree truth and repent of sin to open spiritual gates into the natural realms. Daniel prayed until he experienced breakthrough, empowerment, and revelatory wisdom and knowledge.

PRAYER IS THE GATEWAY

Prayer is the gateway to the realm of vision and dream revelation. Daniel was visited by the angel Gabriel in the vision realm. Gabriel gave Daniel skill with spiritual understanding. It is important to cooperate with the angelic hosts who enable the spiritual eyes of our hearts to be enlightened to see.

It's no wonder that the process we go through to walk in the ways of God's wisdom are forged by fiery tests and trials that fervently conform us to His glorious image. Those with godly insight will understand dream mysteries and use these tools to win souls.

In God's eternal plan to bring salvation to humankind, He deposited His divine light into each person whom He sent into the world. The given measure of divine light is sufficient to draw every man, woman, boy, and girl back into the "Giver of Light." But each person must choose to walk in the light and allow God's light to bring salvation. Those who refuse to walk in the light continue to dwell in darkness and never reach their full potential or God-given destiny. As true light shines in our hearts we are able to remove the things that cause us to stumble.

Dreams and visions bring about a face-to-face encounter similar to what Moses had with God. Dreams show us the goodness of the Lord's countenance upon us. Through our dreams, He places gladness and peace in our hearts; He shows us how to prosper and live in safety.

God supplied the children of Israel with light in their dwellings while the Egyptians cowered in total darkness (see Exod. 10:21-23); He also leads us by His great light. When God lead His children out of Egypt's darkness He went before them as the pillar of cloud by day, and the pillar of fire by night (see Exod. 13:21). God's light was never removed from their presence. This is why we can depend upon the light of His dreams by night, and His enlightenment by day.

Many stumble because there are areas of darkness in their lives they cannot navigate. These dark areas form strongholds that continually resist growth and progress. When the light of God comes into a dream, the dreamer is often able to clearly receive the truth about a situation for the first time, and the truth breaks the power of the lie that has held that person captive (see 1 John 1:5-7).

When we are held in the captivity of darkness, we lose our hope. The Lord circumcises our ears to hear His voice in the night season through our dreams and visions. His prophetic word enters into our bones and spirit to test and transform us. His Word becomes like water bringing healing to our disjointed, dry bones, and He restores us to abundant life.

Dreams can lead us out of darkness and guide us into God's ever-increasing light. One way to know the path to our future is to embrace the dreams God gives. Dreams will indicate the progress we have made and the work and decisions that are necessary to further our life goals (see Phil. 3:12-16).

Truth will continue to confront the dreamer's soul by causing dreams to reoccur until the truth is embraced. Truth has the power to bring the necessary changes to reality, reforming the character and habits of the soul so that we are able to create the godly life we desire. Dreams only seem impossible when we view them through eyes of fear. When we behold their wisdom with eyes of faith they become a living reality of truth. Forgetting and releasing the painful failures in our past helps us move on to a healthier and happier tomorrow.

When we turn to the Lord, we see Him as He is because the veils of limitation are taken away, and deep calls unto deep (see Ps. 42:7). He is calling for us to be reconnected and united with Him—which is the purpose for which we were created (see 2 Cor. 3:16-18). Veils blind our eyes from seeing the spiritual wisdom and apprehending the revelation knowledge dreams bring. Our desire should be to gaze into the glory and hear the Holy Spirit whispering to our heart. We must seek God's wisdom and revelation to unlock the hidden mysteries that He wants to communicate. The Spirit of the Lord enters our dreams to remove the veils from our hearts and faces so that we will be able to see Him in His transcendent beauty. When we see Him, we will be like Him. He is transforming us from one realm of glory into a higher realm of glory as He reveals Himself to us. We cannot behold Him and continue to live in an unchanged state. As He reveals Himself to us, He is coaching us so that we can understand His mysteries.

There is no time or distance in the Spirit realm. God created time and space for us. The Bible states that one day with the Lord is as a thousand years and a thousand years is as one day. The Holy Spirit can cause us to transcend time and space barriers of the past, present, and future in our dreams by imparting glimpses of the spiritual realm as we sleep. Dreams have the ability to take us out of the natural realms of time. They can move us back into the past, help us to deal with the present, or launch us into the future. The past is history, the future is a mystery, and the present is a gift. That's why they call it a present. Dreams ignite the conscious awareness of our physical, emotional, intellectual, social, and spiritual well-being. Dream symbols come from different areas including our present life, past memories, our subconscious and conscious mind.

Dreams give revelation knowledge that enables us to understand the mysteries sealed in God's heart from the beginning of time. God comes into our dreams to show us who He is in all of His magnificent splendor, love, brilliance, and beauty (see Ps. 65:8-9).

Each time we see God for who He is we are transformed more and more into His image. As we sleep, the Lord comes and helps us transcend our sight, hearing, and our natural minds so that we can see revelation by the Holy Spirit. We are given the knowledge and understanding of mysteries and heavenly beings that we have never imagined. The Spirit of the Lord enables us to step out of the natural realm into the boundless existence of eternity. In the dream realm there are no limitations. We can freely move from the present to the past and even look forward into the future.

WHY DREAMS AND VISIONS?

Paul knew the way of the Spirit. He was translated into the heavenly realms. Because this is true, we can experience this too! In Second Corinthians 12:1-4 Paul spoke of receiving visions and revelation from the Lord. He said that being caught up into the *"third heaven,"* and not knowing whether he was in the body or out of the body, was an experience.

He said he experienced "inexpressible things that cannot be put into words, things man is not permitted to tell" (see 2 Cor. 12:4 NIV). He found it difficult to communicate what he saw and experienced in the heavenly realms with his limited vocabulary, and we will too.

John the Revelator was also invited into the realms of the Spirit when he saw a door standing open in Heaven (see Rev. 4:1-2).

John was given an invitation to see the future from a heavenly perspective, but he had to enter the Spirit realm to access the door. Jesus is the door. God is not a respecter of persons. The same invitation that was issued to the apostles Paul and John is being offered to each of us today. So we must learn to navigate the realms of the Spirit in our prayers, dreams, and visions.

God uses dreams to address many issues in our lives to bring us into greater maturity. God's parabolic language in dreams is right in line with the ways He has spoken to people throughout Scripture. We live in a time when Scripture says we will dream dreams, see visions, and prophesy as God pours out His Spirit upon us (see Joel 2:28). The Body of Christ has been given the ability to understand the parables God has hidden in the dreams we dream *and* in the dreams He's given to those who don't know Him yet.

The key to understanding God's dream language is that we must use a biblical basis for interpretation. We rely on the Holy Spirit as our source of revelation, understanding, wisdom, and proper application.

Jesus often taught using parables, which are stories with a deeper spiritual and moral meaning. His disciples asked, *"Why do You speak to them in parables?"* He told them that understanding parables and symbolic imagery is crucial to uncovering the mysteries of the Kingdom (see Matt. 13:10-17). Dreams are basically night parables. The Bible is the first place to look to understand the symbols found in our dreams.

These mysteries are hidden in the realms of the Spirit. Therefore, believers must worship God in Spirit and in truth to enter into this realm of spiritual understanding. It is the Spirit of truth who leads us into all truth (see John 14:17-18).

Dreams are gateways to the supernatural expressions of God. The Holy Spirit comes into our bedchambers to reveal mysteries. There is an urgent call to intimacy with God as never before. The Bible says the marriage bed is undefiled (see Heb. 13:4). You don't let just anyone into the sacred bedchambers—only your covenant lover. Yet, at night the lover of our soul comes to visit us with keys to unlock divine mysteries that are hidden in His heart. He longs to share His secrets with His beloved bride. It is imperative that we learn His love language of dreams. Understanding mysteries of the night will enable us to know His plans and purposes for our life (see Jer. 29:11).

The Holy Spirit comes to reveal the Father and Jesus the Son to us in our dreams (see John 14:23). As we love God whole-heartedly, He will dwell within us and reveal the mysteries of His everlasting Kingdom. Once we understand that God is speaking in our dreams, we will hunger to understand His symbolic language.

Dreams are often a window into divine conversations. Once we learn the symbolic language of dreams, we will begin to walk in an increasing level of understanding of the wisdom being communicated to us. Our God-given dreams hold the answers to the questions we have. Once the correct interpretation is embraced, we have the courage to obey by giving the dream expression.

Deep within the soul of every person is a sense of eternity that can only find fulfillment in knowing God and doing what He created us to do (see Eccles. 3:11).

With God's enlightenment, the dreams we dream become the roadmaps that help direct us to His higher plans. As we call on God, we will begin to comprehend His ways, thoughts, and plans for us revealed in the dreams He gives. Through embracing the changes that our dreams bring, we can walk the new road that God intends for us to walk.

Dreams become the strategic roadmaps that align us with destiny. Dreams contain power that enables us to see what we were created to become. Prophetic dreams reveal God's intended life script, which allows us to walk along His designated path.

The Holy Spirit helps direct the dreamer in His waking life to align with His greatest possible destiny.

Dreams allow us to look carefully at our lives from every angle. When our eyes are opened to the ways God sees things, we can see our destiny and the world around us from His perspective. Spiritual understanding is different than natural wisdom. The presence of the Holy Spirit must be resting upon our natural senses of sight, sound, touch, taste, and smell for us to experience the Spirit realm. *Spiritual wisdom* directs us regarding the future. In contrast, *spiritual knowledge* causes us to reflect back on past experiences (both triumphs and failures) through the eyes of God (see Isa. 43:19-21).

A DIVINE STRATEGY WAITING TO UNFOLD

This higher road may not always be easy, but it leads to maturity in character and fulfillment of our destiny. We choose this higher spiritual road when we decide to go with God by accepting Jesus and the leading of the Holy Spirit. Throughout our life journey, God continually sensitizes our souls to recognize the ways He wants to speak to us. This path enables us to encounter peace, joy, and fulfillment, and it satisfies our desire to be special, successful, and loved. Along the narrow way, each person discovers a divine strategy waiting to unfold in his or her faith walk. Within every soul is a dream that calls each of us to reflect the image and nature of God. It is like a flower yet unfolding. Our life dreams are calling us to emerge from the cocoon, spread our wings, and catch the breath of God's Spirit, the Holy Spirit, so that we can each soar to the highest heights to become the best we were created to be. God knows the path and the course corrections we need to take when our spirit is overwhelmed (see Ps. 142:3a). Soul dreams call us to change by causing us to objectively look at our mind, will, and emotions as they relate to God, our relationships, health, well-being, and prosperity (see John 17:17).

Dreams reveal the truth of where we are, where we are going, and what obstacles we need to remove to get there. Biblical interpretation enables us to unpack the dream and apply its wisdom to our lives. Dreams can help deliver us from destructive life patterns. Instead of going around the mountain one more time, a new track is laid that takes us into a higher reality. God is establishing His Kingdom in our lives, and He is doing it through dreams and visions. The song between the heart of God and the human spirit and soul has many methods of expression: the Bible; a still small voice; an audible voice; visions; circumstantial confirmations; signs and wonders; and the list continues. God speaks to us through dreams to help us become what we are called to be—productive, responsible, successful, prosperous, loved, and fulfilled. God speaks to the human soul through dreams that influence and challenge our very core. As we accept challenges, we are able to grow and mature in many aspects of life. The life we live here on earth is our training ground for eternity. Every day we are faced with decisions and tests we must overcome with the skills and wisdom we have been given. If any of us lack wisdom, we should ask God who will give us His wisdom without measure.

As our understanding is enlightened with God's wisdom we will be able to follow the leading our dreams provide. Life would be so much smaller if we were not able to dream. So dream freely and see God bring to pass increase, largeness, sufficiency, and a grand future.

MORE ABOUT
BARBIE BREATHITT

DR. BARBIE BREATHITT is an author, television guest, ordained minister, dedicated educator, and respected teacher of the supernatural manifestations of God. Barbie's dynamic teaching skills, intelligence, and quick wit keep her a favorite with audiences everywhere. Through prayer, intense study, and years of research, Barbie has become a recognized leader in dream interpretation and has equipped people in more than 40 nations around the globe. Her prophetic gifting and deep spiritual insights have helped people understand the supernatural ways God speaks.

2

PRAYER THE WAY GOD INTENDED

By Scott McDermott

It was a conversation with a man I deeply respected that fueled my quest to understand prayer the way God intended it to be. His words were brief and to the point. "Scott, I see a significant problem in the Church today. People just don't know how to pray." I could hardly believe what I was hearing. Believers who don't know how to pray? How could that be? Most of the believers I knew certainly knew how to pray. Okay, maybe they didn't pray very long, and maybe their prayer life wasn't as consistent as they truly wanted, but they certainly knew how to pray, didn't they? Prayer isn't rocket science. How difficult can prayer really be? Prayer is simple. Tell God what you need, be sure to add at least a mustard seed of faith, and there you have it! You've prayed! The problem is, the more I thought about his comments, the more curious I became. What if he was right? Sometimes God sends people into our lives to plant an important seed. This was one of those moments for me. Little did I know that I was standing on the verge of my own spiritual revolution.

Let me begin by saying that I was not a novice to prayer when I had this conversation. Prayer was a significant part of my life. It was not uncommon for me to wake up at 5 A.M. in order to spend 2 to 3 hours in prayer. By most standards, that would be considered a better than average prayer life. Over the years I had learned to pray in a familiar and consistent pattern. Using the Lord's prayer as my guide, along with a growing list of intercessory requests, I set out each day to cover important ground. Three important assumptions defined how I prayed:

Assumption #1: Prayer is something I am supposed to do. Since I saw prayer as an obligation, prayer was primarily a demonstration of faithfulness and personal discipline for me. If there was a problem in my prayer life, personal discipline could solve it.

Assumption #2: Prayer is the place where I am supposed to cover important ground with God. In practical terms, this meant that my growing list of prayer came to embody and define the important ground I was responsible to cover each day. As my prayer list continued to grow, my daily prayer time became wearisome, difficult, and quite a daunting task.

Assumption #3: Prayer is the place where I earn my approval before God. Because prayer was something I was supposed to do, a place to cover important ground, I felt a growing responsibility for all that was before me. If I didn't meet these expectations, I felt as if I had failed.

These assumptions led to long and tedious prayer times. Still, prayer was a good place for me. I prayed willingly, with great sincerity and consistent discipline. I was always glad when I spent my time alone with the Lord, and I always felt guilty when I missed it. Perhaps that is why this conversation impacted me so powerfully. Now I wondered if my own assumptions were correct. What if there was another way to approach prayer?

FIND A MISSING COMPONENT

I set out to discover what the Bible taught about prayer. Certainly there were many biblical portraits of prayer that confirmed certain aspects of my everyday prayer life. I was relieved to find allusions to set times of prayer (see Rom. 1:10; Phil. 1:4; Eph. 1:16), early morning prayer (Ps. 5:3; 88:13; Mark 1:35), and the consistent call to perseverance in prayer (see Matt. 7:7-8; Luke 18:1). It was, however, the other portraits of prayer that I found to be both disconcerting and enlightening.

One such episode is described in Exodus 33. Having led the Israelites out of Egypt, Moses now found himself in heavy intercession for a rebellious people. Two descriptions of Moses' prayer life seemed to jump off the page. The first description had to do with the way in which Moses' prayer life is described in the text. It was described as "friendship." Exodus 33:11 says *The LORD would speak to Moses face to face, as a man speaks with his friend."* (NIV). Friendship means an intimate relationship combined with a sense of rapport, warmth, and closeness. As much as I loved to pray, I can't say that I would have chosen the word *friendship* to describe my prayer life. My prayer time was more about performance than presence, and more about faithfulness than friendship. When you are simply praying the prayer list, and trying to cover ground, it is all too easy to miss the relational aspect of prayer. It's sort of like sitting at the kitchen table with your spouse and reading a list of things you want your spouse to do for you without ever engaging them in the process. If prayer is relational by nature, then prayer is more than telling God what I want Him to do.

If prayer is a friendship at its core, then the approach to prayer must change. I believe every intercessor will pass through a similar battle. Exodus 33 paints this battle in dramatic fashion. Because of Israel's rebellion, God declares that He will not go with them into the Promised Land. Instead, God will send an angel who will represent Him along the journey and help bring to pass all that He has promised. Israel can have God's promises, but they will not have God's presence. On the surface it does not sound like a bad deal. You can have an angel who represents God and you can have God's promises too. Many have settled for less. Moses, however, is not one to settle for less. He knows the value of God's presence. After a period of wrangling with God, God agrees to go with them. An angel and the promises are not good enough. In verses 15 through 16 Moses declares,

> *...If Your Presence does not go with us, do not send us up from here. How will anyone know that You are pleased with me and with Your people unless You go with us? What else will distinguish me and Your people from all the other people on the face of the earth?* (Exodus 33:15-16 NIV)

On this stage, Moses brings into focus the battle every intercessor will face. Every intercessor must decide whether they will choose God's promises over God's presence. For those who choose God's promises first, they only receive a modicum of fulfillment. Prayer will become a battle for how much I can claim and how much I can produce through prayer. Prayer will be reduced to getting the results I want. But for those who choose God's presence over God's promises, something extraordinary happens. God blesses them by giving both His presence and His promises in greater measure. Abiding gives way to fruitfulness. Presence yields promise. Relationship produces more lasting fruit. It's the test every intercessor will face if they want to be a friend of God.

This initial insight started to revolutionize my prayer life. If prayer is about friendship, then I knew I had to change my initial approach to prayer. For a season I put down the typical prayer pattern and I began to approach God in a much more relational manner. At first I was not quite sure how to do this so I started with something like this: "Father, it's just me. I have just come to be with you. It's not your promises I'm after right now. It's your presence in my life that I want most of all. I just want to be with you." Then I would pause and wait in the silence. The silence became especially meaningful. In it I could feel my heart being re-calibrated from an achievement orientation to a relationship orientation. That's when something wonderful and unexpected began to happen. I began to sense God's presence at the beginning of my prayer time. It didn't come from shouting and jumping up and down as I began my devotional time, though I'm sure a good measure of this would do us all some good. No, it came in just slowing down and acknowledging that I was made for the presence of God. It's been over 26 years now and that little experiment has become a common practice. My prayer time usually begins like this:

"Good morning, Father! It's me. I've come to be with you." Somehow, that little beginning reminds me that my prayer agenda is first of all about God's presence.

GOD SPEAKS

There was still a second element I was yet to discover from this passage in Exodus. Because prayer was relational at its core, I would discover that prayer had a dialogical dimension to it. By that I mean that in prayer God desires to both hear *from me* and speak *to me*. I must confess that this was the greatest surprise of all. Even though I had read Exodus 33 numerous times in the past, I had never noticed the dialogue that took place between Moses and God until now. For Moses, prayer was conversational. As I looked at the Exodus 33:11, I noticed it clearly stated that Moses did more than speak to God. God also spoke to Moses: "*The Lord would **speak** to Moses face to face, as a man **speaks** with his friend*" (Exod. 33:11 NIV).

Moses' dialogue with God was not unique. Numerous biblical narratives contain similar examples of the dialogical nature of prayer. In the life of Paul, for example, we discover just how life-changing one of these moments can be. In Second Corinthians, Paul goes into considerable detail describing the recurring hardships that challenged him on every side throughout his ministry. Pressured, afflicted, perplexed, persecuted, Paul had seen it all. His descriptions are told in a compelling and gripping manner. No spiritual leader can read them without being moved by his dedication and resilience. Yet one theme clearly emerges; Paul had been to the breaking point and lived to tell about it (see 2 Cor. 1:8-10). The only question that begs to be asked is this: How?

How did Paul find this inner tenacity and perseverance to continue? The answer is found in Second Corinthians 12:7-10.

Despite the great revelations that come Paul's way (see 2 Cor. 12:1), there was a "thorn in the flesh" he also experienced. While Paul never provides a clear description of what the thorn in the flesh entailed, it was clearly something he did not want in his life. Three times he sought the Lord to remove it from his life and ministry. Despite his repeated requests, nothing seemed to change. (See Second Corinthians 12:7-9.) Sometimes God's greatest miracles are not found in what He does *for* us but in what He does *to* us. When God decides not to change our circumstances, He decides to change us instead. In response to Paul's prayer, God suddenly and profoundly speaks to Paul. *"My grace is sufficient for you"* (2 Cor. 12:9 NIV). A more literal translation would be "sufficient is my grace for you." The word *sufficient* stands at the forefront of the phrase in the Greek text, highlighting an emphatic message God is conveying to Paul.

By placing the word *sufficient* at the beginning of the sentence, God is underscoring the word He wants Paul to remember. God's grace will be *sufficient*, meaning "enough" or "adequate for a particular purpose."[1] Not only will God's grace and empowering be enough for Paul, the tense of the Greek verb translated as "sufficient" is in a tense that conveys the continuing nature of that sufficiency. In other words, the sufficiency that God is describing *never ends*. God's grace will always be enough! No matter what Paul faces now and forever, God's sufficiency will consistently and continuously abound to Him. One word radically altered Paul's outlook. The thorn that caused him shame would now become a testimony to God's never-failing ability. The thorn that preyed upon Paul's weakness would no longer rule him. God's power always makes itself known best against the backdrop of our limitations. Now that is one life-changing conversation!

I had read these narratives and others many times for many years, but I had never to this point recognized the conversational nature of any of these passages. When I did, I had to concede an important working assumption about biblical prayer: Prayer was a dialogue, not just a monologue. Prayer was the place where God wanted to speak to me as much as I wanted to speak to Him. Practically speaking, this meant that I had to make some adjustments in the way I prayed. My prayer time now had to accommodate the possibility that God wanted to speak to me.

I remember one of my early listening prayer experiences. It was a busy day around the house. We were about to receive some long-awaited, out-of-town guests. Nothing will inspire you more to get your house in order than receiving out-of-town company. That meant our house went on high alert. Rooms had to be readied, floors vacuumed, end tables dusted, beds freshly made, everything made to look the way it is supposed to and better. My wife Dawn was quickly caught up in the pressure of making our home look both presentable and welcoming. For me, it just did not seem so stressful. While she frantically dashed about the home cleaning, straightening, and decorating, I quietly withdrew and sequestered myself into my study for a time of prayer. Closing the door behind me, I felt a sense of relief and escape. My study was my refuge from the world. Once I closed the door, everyone in our home knew that I was not to be disturbed. I was having time with God. So I was safe for a time, or so I thought.

I began my prayer time once again in pursuit of a new relationship with God. "Oh Father, it's me. I have just come to be with you." I waited for a moment, quieting myself before the Lord.

In the stillness and quietness a picture came to my mind of my wife frantically running around the house, filled with stress and anxiety. The picture itself was atypical. Dawn is the quiet type. She seldom displays emotion of any kind and certainly not much, if any, frustration. Even in the most difficult of times, I have known her to be a reservoir of peace. So the picture quite frankly surprised me. I immediately surmised that God was directing me to begin praying for Dawn.

Sensing what I thought was the Spirit's direction, I prayed, "Lord, give her grace. Help her, Lord. Give her the strength she needs. Bring her peace and freedom." I paused because I felt a bit of a check in my spirit over the prayer. I backed up and tried again. "Lord, you know how my wife is so caught up with all she has to do. Lord, she needs help. Please send her the help she needs. She is such a blessing to me." I paused and listened again, waiting for the witness of my spirit to my prayer. It was the pause that did it. My mind began to replay the words I had just prayed, "Lord, send her the help she needs...Lord, send her the help she needs...Lord, send her the help she needs." I could feel the growing conviction in this one brief pause which soon gave way to some heavenly advice. "Scott, what are you doing here? She is your wife. Go out there and help her." It's convicting when you are the answer to your own prayer. If we are willing to listen, prayer can be dangerous.

That was one of my early experiences in learning how to hear the voice of God. But over the years I have been amazed at the clarity God has brought to me in pausing, listening, and praying. As my relationship with God grew, so did my own self-disclosure to God. Just as Moses and Paul shared their inner frustrations and questions with God, I began to do the same.

Just as they paused and listened, I did the same. My prayer list became a prayer conversation. Sometimes, I would hear the still small voice. Sometimes, I would see a picture which helped clarify how to pray. Sometimes, I would be led to a verse of Scripture. Other times, I heard nothing but silence, but even the silence reminded me that He was still God (see Ps. 46.10): To my surprise, my motivation for prayer began to change. The revolution had begun. Prayer became more than a discipline; it was something I longed for. I noticed that when I missed my prayer time I no longer felt guilty. I felt hungry. Missing prayer was like missing a meal. Prayer became life and not just a requirement. Prayer was life because I was truly finding the presence of God. But there was another connection that still needed to be made. There was a benefit that I was yet to see and understand.

MINISTRY AND THE SECRET PLACE

Have you ever wondered what the connection is between your own personal devotional life and how God uses you in ministry? I have. I suppose up to this point I viewed the connection of personal prayer time to ministry in this way: The more I prayed personally, the more prayer credit I accrued. The more personal time I spent in prayer, the more favor I earned. It was sort of like putting coins in a jar. The more time I prayed, the more the coins accumulated, the more I had to spend. My perspective was not uncommon. Many seem to view their personal prayer time as the place to earn the favor of God. This is especially true in ministry. I had heard it said many times over that if you want a fruitful ministry you must pray more. The more hours you pray, the bigger and more powerful your ministry will become. Little wonder I came to perceive that personal prayer time was about accrued credit rather than something else. That perspective was about to change.

I was teaching a seminar on spiritual gifts from the Book of First Corinthians. The group I was teaching was hungry to learn all I knew about the subject. The fact was, I knew very little at the time. Much of what I had learned came from books, seminars, and the experiences of others. In preparing for the presentation, I had read the entire Book of First Corinthians. Here Paul describes the Church and its individual members as the temple of God. On the one hand, the word *temple* conveyed the idea of holiness, separateness, and consecration. On the other hand, *temple* implied God's presence. In Old Testament history, the temple represented God's living presence among the Israelites. At the temple's consecration described in First Kings 8:11, for example, God's glory was so great that the priests could not enter the temple to perform their duties. By the time of the New Testament, we are told that God is building a new temple, but unlike the Old Testament temple, this one was not made with bricks and mortar, but made with people (see 1 Cor. 3:16; Eph. 2:21; 1 Peter 2:4). God has always wanted a people who would carry His presence on earth (see Exod. 33:16). The Church, as God's called-out and set-apart people, are carriers of His presence (see 1 Cor. 6:19). Church is to be a place where God is at home with us and we are home with God. It is little wonder then, that Paul spends considerable time teaching on what it means to worship together in the presence of God. Where God's presence is, you can expect amazing things to happen. The manifestation of spiritual gifts is one of those amazing things.

Walking my way verse by verse through First Corinthians 12, my teaching moved to practical application. Specifically, I shared the importance of not hurrying when praying for others. We must learn to *slow down, pause,* and carefully *listen* to what God might be saying to us so that we can pray more effectively. Sometimes God gives us pictures, sometimes God speaks to us through small impressions, sometimes God speaks in a still small voice, while other times there just seems to be an inner knowing and deep confidence in what we are praying into. Suddenly, in the middle of my teaching, I saw a common connection I had never seen before. There was a clear connection between the way God speaks to us in prayer ministry and the way God speaks to us in our own personal prayer life. It's not the methods that change, it's just the context. "Of course," I thought, "that makes perfect sense." My personal prayer time and prayer ministry are similar at the core because the ministry of the Spirit flows out of relationship with God.

This was a radical association for me, and quite frankly I was shocked that I had never heard anyone teach on it. While in the past I had viewed my time alone with God as time to accrue enough credit to be used by God, I now saw my personal prayer time as the place in which I learned to host and discern the presence of God. This had untold benefits. Prayer was no longer the place where I earned God's favor; prayer became the place where I received God's favor. Personal prayer became the place where God equipped me for ministry because it was there that God tuned my spirit to discern the sound of His voice. The more I learned to become a person of God's presence when I was alone, the more I could recognize His presence and His voice at the place of ministry to others. One was a natural outflow of another. That was prayer the way God intended it to be.

Over the years, I have been truly astounded at the things that have happened at the place of ministry. While recently doing some ministry in a different country, I found myself ministering to a small gathering of very committed believers. I had never met them before, and aside from the obvious fact that we were strangers to each other, there was a language barrier as well. However, the sense of cultural and language distance soon evaporated as the worship began. Their worship was rich and meaningful, demonstrating their singled-minded commitment to Jesus. In this country, commitment to Jesus came at some cost, and I was deeply moved by their example. I was the guest teacher for this small gathering, and after sharing a brief teaching on how God walks us through the healing of our hearts, I felt impressed to ask if I could pray for each one of them.

I made my way over to the first person who, unbeknownst to me, was visiting the group for the first time. Through an interpreter I asked her to stand and I placed my hand upon her shoulder, paused and listened. As I paused, pictures came to my mind relating to her life. I could see her crying alone in her room. I could sense some of the life situations that challenged her. In my spirit, I asked God to show me how to pray about what I was sensing. In humility and faith, I began to pray into her life and into the pictures I was seeing. My words were not directional. They were encouraging, comforting, and intended to build her up. As I looked at her face, I could see tears forming in her eyes and gently streaming down her face. God's Word was stirring her heart. We were in a sacred place. We were in the presence of God. God was opening up the pain of her life and lifting her burden.

I then moved to the next person and then the next until I finished praying for everyone in the room. Two hours had passed and I was unaware of what was happening in the conversations around the room as I was praying. An interpreter began to share the nature of their conversations. They were saying: "Truly this must be God." "There is no way he could have known all these details about each one of our lives if God had not told him." Faith was filling the room. Expectation grew with each passing prayer, and most of all, God was changing lives. It was a good day of ministry. We continued in prayer for another hour. I didn't know any of their situations before I came into their meeting that day. Only God knew. God just chose to use a vessel who longs to stay within the sound of his voice, and for that I am grateful. I have seen this scenario play itself out time and time again everywhere I have ministered. I am humbled by it, but at the same time, with each passing encounter my faith grows. I can't wait to pray for people just to see what God does. Praying for others is exciting.

I am thankful for all that has happened to me since I began praying this way over 26 year ago. I have experienced a spiritual revolution. What about those assumptions I had about prayer? Well, they have changed somewhat. Prayer is no longer something I am supposed to do it really is something I long to do. I still value getting up early and spending my hours in prayer, but the motivation has changed. Prayer is the most refreshing part of my day. I cannot wait to be with the Lord. What about covering important ground in prayer? Oh yes, I still cover important ground, I still stand in the gap and, I must confess, I still have my list. I am just not bound to it any longer. Instead, I listen to what God has to say about my list. I listen to what He has to say to me and what He might want me to do in response to the needs that are before me. But most importantly, I am no longer driven by performance to earn God's favor. Prayer is a relationship for me now, and with each passing year, it does grow even richer. So what has changed? Everything!

I have come to believe that prayer is the birthplace of the will of God on earth. Heaven touches earth first at the place of prayer making prayer an essential component for Kingdom advancement. This heavenly pursuit is not merely me bringing my agenda to God. I share in a partnership with God. I come to God, but God also comes to me. That has made all the difference.

ENDNOTE

1. J.P. Louw, & E.A. Nida. (1996, c1989). *Greek-English lexicon of the New Testament: Based on semantic domains* (electronic ed. of the 2nd edition.) (1:598). New York: United Bible Societies.

~ ~

MORE ABOUT
DR. SCOTT MCDERMOTT

Scott McDermott has served as the Lead Pastor at the Crossing in Washington Crossing, Pennsylvania, since 1993. During that time, he has seen this congregation miraculously touched by God's renewing and restoring grace. He also holds a Ph.D. in New Testament Studies.

3

THE PURPOSE OF THE PROPHETIC VOICE

By Dr. Jane Hamon

The young lady in the back of the room seemed to be very uncomfortable in the spiritual atmosphere as I was speaking about hearing the voice of God. "Jesus said in John 10:27, 'My sheep hear My voice,'" I declared. She began to fidget as I said, "His expectation is for every believer to cultivate a relationship with Him that involves both us speaking to God in prayer, as well as Him communicating back to us by His voice, the Holy Spirit." As I spoke these words, the young lady seemed to have had enough of this kind of talk and got up and left the room. I quietly heard the Holy Spirit say to me, "She will be back, and when she sits down again, prophesy to her."

A few minutes passed and the young lady did in fact return to the service. So I asked her if I could minister to her. She looked shocked, then shrugged her shoulders and said, "Whatever," and came forward. What I didn't realize is that she had excused herself to go into the ladies restroom. There, she later told me, she was pacing back and forth saying, "I don't believe any of this prophetic stuff. I don't think it's real, and as a matter of fact, God, I don't even think You are real. All my life I have asked You question after question, and You have never answered me. God, if You are real, prove it to me!" Then she came back into the meeting and sat down, and I said, "May I minister to you?"

I had no idea what had just transpired in her conversation toward God, but as I laid my hands on her and listened to the Lord, He had me speak these words: "My daughter you've had question after question that you don't feel I have ever answered. And because I am God, I don't have to prove Myself to you, but because I love you I *will* prove myself to you…." The prophecy went on to address many of the things about her life that she had often wondered about. Big tears began to flow down her face as she heard not only God's voice, but His heart expressed toward her.

Later, after the meeting, this young lady shared what had transpired. I obviously did not have any idea why the word affected her on such a deep level; yet, she felt her life had been completely changed. Her comment to me was, "Today I found out that God is real!" Catching God's voice will make Him real to us individually, but it also empowers us to make Him real to others who may not yet know Him as He longs to be known.

We are living in times of great restoration and outpouring in the earth. These are times of reformation—times in which God is re-ordering His Church to produce a greater demonstration of the Kingdom by releasing His voice in the midst of the earth. God is reforming us so that we can *make Him real* to a lost and dying world.

THE REVELATION KEY

When someone has a key, he or she has the ability to start a car, to unlock a building, or to lock up a treasure. Keys either release or deny access to specific things in the earth. So it is with spiritual keys. When one has a spiritual key, he or she can open things that have been locked or lock things that have been opened. Spiritual keys give access to the powers of the heavenly Kingdom to make available all resources from that realm.

Jesus spoke of the keys of the Kingdom of God, one of which is the key of revelation. One day Jesus asked His disciples, "Who do men say that I am?" Many of them had some reasonable answers, but Peter had a revelation from God: "You are the Christ, the son of the living God" he declared. Jesus replied "Blessed are you Simon Bar Jonah, for flesh and blood did not reveal this to you, but this revelation came from you hearing the voice of my Father in Heaven" (author's paraphrase, see Matt. 16:16-17). Jesus then went on to proclaim, "You are Peter and on *this rock* I will build My Church, and the very gates of hell will not be able to prevail against it!" (author's paraphrase, see Matt. 16:18). Jesus was not saying that He would build the Church upon Peter, but upon the rock. This rock is the foundational truth that God's desire is to release His voice of revelation to us, and once we receive it, the very gates of hell will not be able to stand against us.

Jesus then went on to declare, "*I will give you the keys of the kingdom of heaven; whatever you bind* [lock up] *on earth will be bound* [locked up] *in heaven, and whatever you loose* [unlock] *on earth will be loosed* [unlocked] *in heaven*" (Matt. 16:19 NIV). The key of revelation will take us past the reasoning of our natural mind and bring us into a supernatural perspective that we might accomplish God's Kingdom purposes in the midst of the earth (see Matt. 16:13-18).

After Jesus' resurrection, He revealed Himself to His disciples for forty days. Before He ascended to His heavenly throne, He wanted to put keys into the hands of His disciples. "Go back to Jerusalem and wait for the Promise of the Father...for you shall receive power when the Holy Ghost has come upon you" (authors paraphrase, see Acts 1:4-8). Jesus knew that the disciples would need a supernatural empowerment to take His message into the entire world.

The disciples returned to Jerusalem to wait for God's promise. As the wind of God blew in, and the fire of God fell, each one was baptized with the Holy Spirit and began to speak in other tongues.

It was a powerful time of impartation upon this small group of believers who would eventually turn the world upside down.

That day, a great revival broke out in Jerusalem. Peter then got up and decreed the prophecy from Joel. *"...in the last days...I will pour out of my spirit on all flesh."* Peter was proclaiming that this was the fulfillment of an ancient prophecy. He continued, *"...Your sons and your daughters shall prophesy, your young men shall see visions, your old men shall dream dreams. And on My menservants and on My maidservants I will pour out My spirit...And they shall prophesy"* (Acts 2:17-18 NKJV).

Peter was declaring to the people that God was pouring out His Spirit and the result would be people hearing and speaking revelation from the voice of God. The word *prophecy* simply means "God is speaking." Peter was saying, "God is giving us the key of revelation today, whether through dreams, visions, or simply by hearing the voice of the Lord."

Today, we are in another time of great outpouring of the Holy Spirit in the earth. God is not only saving people from their sins, but also empowering them through the baptism of the Holy Spirit so that they can hear the voice of God to release His Kingdom into the earth. Millions of believers have received this baptism with the evidence of speaking in other tongues. However, many didn't recognize that not only did they acquire a prayer language, but also a mantle of power and revelation. It should be a natural part of our supernatural walk with the Lord to hear His voice, speak what He is saying, and move in His miraculous power.

Hearing God's prophetic voice is not a sideline issue. If we were to remove every Scripture from the Bible that has to do with hearing God's voice through dreams, visions, angelic interaction, prophets, or even through the still, small voice of the Holy Spirit, we would lose almost half the biblical text! God loves to speak! Throughout the pages of Scripture, God reveals Himself as the God that longs to communicate with His people.

As prophetic people are arising throughout the earth, we must recognize that God longs to speak so that He can accomplish His purposes. My husband Tom was raised in a small town in Oklahoma. Tom says that when he was a boy, his father would tell him to do something, and he often didn't move fast enough or respond to his father's voice. His dad would then say, "Boy, I'm not just talking to hear my teeth rattle!" Tom says that when he heard that, he knew he'd better get on the move. Well, our Father God isn't talking just to hear His teeth rattle. There is something He wants us to do when He speaks. So let's look at some of the purposes for God's prophetic voice being released so that we can get on the move as well.

GOD'S VOICE PROMOTES HIS PLAN

God is a strategist and always has a plan. While it is true that His ways are higher than our ways, He also loves to let people in on His plans. Amos 3:7 says, *"Surely the Lord GOD will do nothing, but He revealeth His secret unto His servants the prophets"* (KJV). We can see this in the twenty-ninth book of Jeremiah when the prophet is telling the elders of the Jews, who have been carried into Babylonian captivity, that God has a plan. He tells them, "You are going to be in captivity for seventy years, and though this may seem a hard thing, if you pray for the city I have brought you to, I can still give you peace and prosperity in the midst of your time of captivity. But at the end of the seventy years, I will bring you home to your land" (author's paraphrase, see Jer. 29). He speaks these words of comfort to them in one of the most difficult days of their nation's history. *"'For I know the plans I have for you,' declares the LORD, 'plans to prosper you and not to harm you, plans to give you hope and a future"* (Jer. 29:11 NIV).

God always has a plan and will speak that plan to those who are listening for His voice. Even in the middle of some of the most challenging situations one may face, God has a plan to give you peace and prosperity in your difficulty and bring you out of your captivity and into your divine destiny.

In the Old Testament, God limited His voice to speaking only to a prophet here or there. But we are living in a different day. Today, God is pouring His Spirit out on each of us, and we can all hear His voice. Yes, there are still those whom God has gifted and anointed as prophets to speak His divine plans and purposes into the earth. But there is also an entire company of prophetic people, who are filled with His Spirit, who have learned to listen for His voice, and follow His plan.

As a young girl of 16 years old, I was praying and seeking the Lord regarding my future. At that point in time, my plans for myself included traditional college and then perhaps some sort of career in media or communications. But an encounter with God's voice changed the course of my life and set me on my path of purpose. That day God told me that my plans were not His plans for my life, but that He was calling me into a place of full-time ministry. He clearly told me to go to bible college where I would meet my husband and that the two of us would travel the nations of the world preaching His Word. He said that my husband would preach at times and that I would preach at times, but that He would use us together as a ministry team.

At this point, I had only been a believer for two years and had never had any exposure to women preaching. It seemed to be impossible. Yet the voice of God was so clear and distinct that I shifted my plans to align with His plans. The following year, at the mature age of 17, I went off to bible college. The very first day on campus, I met the man who would become my husband.

Fast forward 30 years, and we have been serving the Lord as the Senior Pastors of Christian International Family Church in Santa Rosa Beach, Florida, for 25 years and have traveled to over 50 nations preaching the Word of God. At times, my husband preaches, and at times I preach. The prophetic word set a course for my life and fulfillment of God's destiny and plan. Clearly, the voice of the Lord is released so that we understand the unique, special, and specific plans and purposes for which we have been created.

GOD'S VOICE PROCLAIMS THE PROMISE

David was the youngest of his father's eight sons. His brothers were men of strength and stature while David was serving his father as a lowly shepherd. But one day David received a prophetic promise that changed the course of his life.

The prophet Samuel had come to Jesse's house, under the direction of the Holy Spirit, to anoint the new king of Israel. The problem was that Israel already had a king, a man named Saul, but the Lord had removed His hand from his life and leadership. Because of this, Samuel was instructed by the Lord to travel to Bethlehem and anoint the new king, and that he would be found in Jesse's house. (See First Samuel 16.)

Upon arrival, Samuel asked to meet Jesse's sons. The oldest son, Eliab, looked like a king. He was tall and good-looking and, just as Samuel prepared to anoint him, God's voice interrupted and said, "This isn't the one." The next son came, and the next, but none of the sons present were the one God wanted Samuel to anoint as king. Finally, after the last son came before Samuel, he asked, "Do you have any other sons?" Jesse replied, "There's David, my youngest. He's out tending the sheep." So Samuel said, "Well, bring the boy here!" As he laid his eyes on the young teenage boy, Samuel heard God's voice say, "This is the one!" Upon hearing this, Samuel anointed David as the future king of Israel declaring that, "Man looks at the outward appearance, but God looks upon the heart."

That day, David received the promise from God regarding his future. But he understood something by the Spirit of God; in order to fulfill the promise, he would have to go through the process. Realizing this, David did not go out and have "King David" business cards printed up immediately. He knew that if this were to take place it would require patience and persistence to obtain the promise.

The next time we hear of David is when he goes to the battlefield to bring his brothers supplies during their confrontation with Goliath of Gath. This man was an intimidating giant who had all of Israel trembling with fear. But when David heard his threats, declarations from the Spirit of God rose up within him. "Who is this uncircumcised Philistine that he should defy the armies of the living God?" he cried. Armed only with a slingshot and the promise of God over his life, David ran to the battle. (See First Samuel 17.)

Today, many people in the Body of Christ are running in battle. Unfortunately, they are running the wrong way! The plan of the enemy is to threaten and intimidate believers into a place of fear or passivity to keep them out of a place of victory. But when one catches God's voice and receives the promise, it enables believers to see things from a different perspective—through the eyes of vision and faith—rather than through the perspective of confusion and fear.

That day David won a mighty victory over Goliath in the sight of all Israel. As a result, he married the king's daughter and moved into the palace. I can almost hear him saying, "Now I know how the prophetic promise about me becoming king is going to come to pass. I will inherit the throne from my father-in-law one day. This will be easy!" Yet, as we all know, this was not how the prophetic word would be fulfilled.

Over time, Saul grew increasingly jealous of David and tried to kill him. David had to flee for his life, leaving behind the palace, but holding on to his promise. Many people with a prophetic promise have to leave things behind from the past season in order to reach forward to possess the future.

In the next several years, David went through the process of running for his life, hiding out in caves, raising an army of men who would defend the land of Israel from intruders, and remaining faithful to God's promise. Even when given the opportunity to kill Saul, which would seemingly hasten the fulfillment of the prophecy, David followed God's principles and refused to touch God's anointed to promote himself. (See First Samuel 24.) He knew that God was the one that gave him the promise and that God would have to be the one to bring it to pass. Through all the time, tests, and trials David kept the promise of God before his eyes until the day when all his dreams came true.

Catching God's voice will result in one receiving a promise from the Father; however, it does not mean that everything will be smooth and easy from that point forward. David's prophetic word catapulted him into one of the most challenging seasons of his life. Others in Scripture found themselves in the same situation. Joseph received a promise from God in the form of two dreams. The next thing he knew, Joseph was being sold into slavery by his brothers. Psalm 105:19 tells us that the word of the Lord tried Joseph. Joseph went from being positioned as a slave to being thrown in prison. But the promise from the Lord from years before kept him positioned in faith until he received the promise. (See Genesis 41.) Hebrews 10:35 tells us not to throw away our confidence and hope, for after we have persevered and done God's will, we will receive the promise.

Don't give up on the promise, even in the face of a trying process. After all the years of slavery and bondage, it only took God one day to move Joseph from the prison to the palace to become prime minister to the Pharaoh in the greatest empire of that time. God knows how to watch over His promise to perform it, but we must stay in His process.

GOD'S VOICE POSITIONS US THROUGH PROPER PERSPECTIVE

There are times when we catch the voice of God and He reveals something new to us about our life, our direction, or our future. Like road signs, these words from God may tell us to make the turn ahead and enter a time of change. Or perhaps, even as God spoke to Abram when he was living in Haran, God had to tell him that he had walked past the promise land and he needed to turn around, do a U-turn, and go back. There are other times that God chooses to encourage us by giving us a confirming word that keeps us on course with His plans: "Destination—straight ahead," or perhaps, "Caution: Bumps in the Road." God's voice positions our faith to understand what God is doing in us and helps us to maintain a positive, proper perspective even during times of challenge or trial.

Years ago, I had a dream in which someone had pulled all the grass out of my yard and replaced it with row after row of turnip greens. I woke up trying to remember if I'd had pizza for dinner the night before, because surely this was a pizza dream! But an hour later, as I was walking from the parking lot into our local grocery store, a little old man approached me and asked, "Do you want to buy some turnip greens?" It startled me after just having had this dream. So I went back to my car and asked the Lord if He was trying to say something to me about turnip greens.

The first thing I must say is that I detest the taste of turnip greens! Was God telling me that I had to start eating turnip greens? Not at all (whew!). What He said to me is that He was bringing me into a time of plucking up things that were pleasant and comfortable (symbolized by the beautiful grass) and replacing them with things that I wouldn't like, but would be good for me (those would be the turnip greens). Yuk!

Though I wasn't excited about the message from this dream, I began to realize this was exactly what God was doing. Through the years, I had clearly told the Lord that there were things that I would "never" do. These "nevers" were my turnip greens.

I had some previous experience with these "never" declarations. By this point, I should have learned to never say "never" to God. When I graduated from high school, knowing there was a call from God upon my life, I told the Lord that there were two things I "never" wanted to be. The first thing that I never wanted to be was a secretary, and the second thing I never wanted to be was a pastor's wife. After I graduated from Bible College, I became a secretary until I became a pastor's wife! Perhaps when we say "never" to God, He takes it as a personal challenge!

So now the Lord was dealing with me about some other things that I had told Him I would "never" do. He had started requiring me to step into some new responsibilities; yet, in my discomfort, I had begun placing limitations on how He could use me. Because He had sent me His Word in a dream and interpretation,

I understood the season I was in and could embrace His process rather than fighting against it.

God is faithful to send us words that will encourage us to stay on the right path and keep a godly perspective. Since I knew that all the discomfort I was going through was not because God was trying to be mean to me, but because in His infinite wisdom He knew it would be good for me, it was much easier to yield to His plans. Catching the voice of God helps us to keep our heart in alignment with the heart of God and maintain His perspective in the midst of trying times.

GOD'S VOICE IS POWERFUL!

Having been a participator in active prophetic ministry for over twenty-five years, I have witnessed many miracles that have come as a result of a person catching God's voice. Psalms 29 is full of descriptive, miraculous occurrences that take place in the earth at the very sound of the voice of the Lord.

We must recognize that God's voice is not restricted to some booming voice from Heaven as was heard the day of Jesus' baptism proclaiming, *"This is my beloved Son, in whom I am well pleased"* (Matt. 3:17 KJV). Today, God has chosen to release His voice through the mouths of His prophets as well as through the mouths of believers everywhere. When this happens, miracles take place.

In the beginning, God released His voice and the heavens and the earth were created. As we study God's creative power in Scripture, we see that God used a prophet to speak to the Shunamite woman who was barren. That prophetic word had the power of creative life, for a few months later her barrenness was broken and she gave birth to a son. God's voice is powerful!

One day while traveling home from a ministry trip, I was on an airplane seated next to a man who had obviously had too much to drink. He kept trying to strike up a conversation with me, but because I wasn't interested in speaking with him, I was giving him short monosyllable answers. Suddenly, I heard the voice of the Lord whisper to me, "Put your book down and talk to the man." So I engaged in conversation with him.

In a few minutes, he asked me what I did for a living. I replied that I was a minister. Well, this infuriated him! He began to shout at me, "A minister! A minister! Well, you are just a…." Do you get the picture? While he was shouting, I began to explain to the Lord that He was the one that asked me to speak with this man. So I asked the Lord, "Why is he so angry?" Quickly, the Lord showed me through a word of knowledge that a priest had abused him as a boy. Secondly, I was shown that he had recently lost a son to a cult.

After he got done shouting, I began to speak to him about the heart of God. I said, "Wow! You sound pretty angry. But as you were 'sharing your heart with me' I asked God why, and I believe He said to tell you that the priest that harmed you as a boy was not representing His heart of love for you and that He is so sorry for all you endured. He also said to tell you that He is also grieved about the path your son has taken, but that He will take care of him and he is alright."

The man's mouth dropped open in astonishment. "Who are you?" he asked me. I replied, "I'm just a Christian that believes that God still wants to speak to us today and I believe He wants you to know how much He loves you." The man dropped his head into his hands and began to sob. "Tell me more about this God, because I don't think I know anything about Him," he cried. For the next hour and a half, I was able to share the truth of the Gospel with this man, who turned out to be a wealthy CEO of a major corporation. He was searching for truth, and he was able to hear it for the first time that day because he caught God's voice.

It's time for believers everywhere to catch the voice of God. As we learn to hear His voice, He will set our lives on paths of purpose, keep us in alignment with His promise, bring us clear, godly perspective in the midst of our challenges, and release His power to and through us to fulfill His plan in the midst of the earth. Listen! He is speaking to you now!

MORE ABOUT
DR. JANE HAMON

JANE HAMON is a prophetic leader who brings life and vision to many through her inspiring messages and through releasing the word of the Lord to individuals, churches, and nations. She and her husband, Tom, are the Senior Pastors at Christian International Family Church, in Santa Rosa Beach, Florida.

4

THE GLORY

By Jason Westerfield

One day while praying to God about what He was going to be doing in our generation, I went into a dream-like state while awake. The Spirit of God was upon me in such a heavy way that my soul and body became completely rested. At this point, my spiritual eyes and ears were open and the inner person of my heart was set free from the limitations of my body as well as space, time, and physical matter.

This glorious rest and liberty was the most amazing experience as God's tangible glory and love coursed through every cell of my being. I was completely in the realm of the Spirit having union with God. The Lord began to speak to me audibly of things to come for this generation and began to show me events that He had predestined for these times that would unfold on the Earth.

The Spirit of God lifted me up into our galaxy with a full view of thousands of stars. As I was peering out in amazement and awe, a long beautiful object with a tail-like ending passed before my eyes. I asked the Lord, "What is this object?" The Lord responded, "It is a comet, son, and is a sign of the times you live in on planet Earth." The Lord then continued, "NASA doesn't know about this comet. It is a sign of the Reformation!"

Immediately, I was taken back through time in the Spirit to the early 1500s. I watched as a young man nailed papers to the door of a building. I asked the Lord, "Who is this man that you are showing me?" The Lord responded, "This young man is Martin Luther and your generation lives in the same season of the Spirit as his did; it is a season of Reformation!" The Lord continued, "He brought a revelation of salvation by faith through grace and not by dead works, and the priesthood of all believers. Your generation is going to go from an understanding of the Church to a revelation of the Kingdom of God!" The Lord also said, "There is a special grace in your generation to walk in a closer, more intimate relationship with Me and walk in the greater works of Jesus with a restored spirit of dominion."

After all of these things occurred, and the Lord had finished showing me what He wanted to reveal to me, I became more aware of my surroundings in this natural temporal realm.

I immediately shared this information with numerous leaders and people. After a few months had passed, I received a phone call from Bill and Beni Johnson of Bethel Church in Redding, California. They asked me if I remembered the word I shared about the comet. I replied that I did and shared the word again. After we finished discussing the word, they shared that NASA had just announced a surprise discovery of a new comet and that the newspaper had written an article about it. The newspaper article wrote that the last time this comet had been seen was in the early 1600s. The early 1600s was the tail end of the Reformation!

The above is a true story of modern-day revelation and prophecy fulfilled with incredible signs and wonders in the heavens. The experience and means of which revelation was received is known as an open-heavens experience and a trance and takes place while in the promised rest of the Lord.

In this glorious kingdom realm of the Spirit, as God leads, you can go to and fro from one place of the earth or universe to another at the speed of a thought. You can also go into higher realms and dimensions outside of this universe going up and down. In the realm of the Spirit, we are not bound to space-time or the physical properties and elements that consist in natural matter.

The first place in the Bible where we find this deep rest from God is in the Book of Genesis with Adam:

> *And the LORD God caused a deep sleep to fall on Adam, and he slept; and He took one of his ribs, and closed up the flesh in its place. Then the rib which the LORD God had taken from man He made into a woman, and He brought her to the man. And Adam said: "This is now bone of my bones and flesh of my flesh; she shall be called Woman, because she was taken out of Man"* (Genesis 2:21-23 NKJV).

It was actually this type of supernatural deep sleep and rest that came from God that God put on Adam to make the first woman. This is also the first recorded surgery ever done as Adam's side had to close up and heal from being opened up by God. Notice the similarity with doctors today. When someone is going to have a significant surgery the doctor will put him to sleep with anesthesia.

When we are having services and the glory of God comes in such a significant way, it is weighty and heavy and becomes difficult to stand. The Spirit of God is getting poured out in substantial measure all over our flesh. All you want to do is lie down, rest, and be with God. During these times of supernatural rest from God, the heavens are open corporately over the body of people. People begin to experience freedom in their spirits and the glory of God begins to rise and shine within them with God's life and light by His Holy Spirit. God will often take people into an open-heavens experience where their spiritual eyes and ears are open to hear God and their hearts turn to Him to be healed. We hear numerous reports of people being taken to Heaven and seeing God and angels or translated other places to see what God wants them to see.

Thousands of people are healed of sickness and disease and scars are removed. This happens as God's life and light, by His Spirit, strengthens their mortal body while being saturated by the overshadowing presence and rest of God. John 1:4 says, *"In Him was Life, and the Life was the Light of men."* Psalm 23:2 says, "The Lord gives His beloved rest and makes us to lie down in green pastures and He leads us beside the still waters" (author's paraphrase).

> *"There remains therefore a rest for the people of God. For he who has entered His rest has himself also ceased from his works as God did from His. Let us therefore be diligent to enter that rest..."* (Hebrews 4:9-11 NKJV).

In the Old Testament, we read that Moses did not want to go forward any farther unless God's *presence and rest went with him.*

Exodus 24:16 states, *"Now the glory of the lord rested on Mount Sinai, and the cloud covered it six days. And on the seventh day He called to Moses out of the midst of the cloud* (NKJV)." All throughout the Bible, we find this glorious rest as God's presence rests so heavily upon the people and the land.

We see this in Second Chronicles 5:13-14. The house of the Lord was filled with a cloud so that the priests could not continue ministering because of the cloud; for the glory of the Lord filled the house of God.

We can worship and pray into such a high place of God's presence and rest that His glory cloud will cover us like a blanket. His glory will continue to flow and pour over us until it becomes difficult to stand any more and all we want to do is lay down. It is at these moments where we surrender and receive all God has laid up for us in the heavens. As we lay down in rest, God fills us with His fullness and abundance.

It is at this point that the weight begins to become so heavy and restful that we are more conscious of God and His abundant love for us than all of our surroundings. He has fully captured our heart, mind, emotions, and all of our attention. This is the place of rest where someone goes out into the Spirit or falls into a trance. Your soul and spirit are caught up in the glory of God. It is also the place where the heavens begin to open and the curtain veil over our heart and mind begins to roll away and the door of our heart opens to the realm of the Spirit. The eyes of our understanding get open to see, hear, encounter, and go with God. This is what the apostle Paul was praying would happen for the believers in Christ at the church of Ephesus.

For this reason, because I have heard of your faith in the Lord Jesus and your love toward all the saints (the people of God), I do not cease to give thanks for you, making mention of you in my prayers. [For I always pray to] the God of our Lord Jesus Christ, the Father of glory, that He may grant you a spirit of wisdom and revelation [of insight into mysteries and secrets] in the [deep and intimate] knowledge of Him, by having the eyes of your heart flooded with light, so that you can know and understand the hope to which He has called you, and how rich is His glorious inheritance in the saints (His set-apart ones), and [so that you can know and understand] what is the immeasurable and unlimited and surpassing greatness of His power in and for us who believe as demonstrated in the working of His mighty strength, which He exerted in Christ when He raised Him from the dead and seated Him at His [own] right hand in the heavenly [places] (Ephesians 1:15-20).

This is also the place from which Jesus would minister by the Holy Spirit. He would see and hear what the Father was doing in Heaven, so He would be able to minister the Kingdom of His Father as a Son *of* the Kingdom.

So Jesus answered them by saying, I assure you, most solemnly I tell you, the Son is able to do nothing of Himself (of His own accord); but He is able to do only what He sees the Father doing, for whatever the Father does is what the Son does in the same way [in His turn]. The Father dearly loves the Son and discloses to (shows) Him everything that He Himself does. And He will disclose to Him (let Him see) greater things yet than these, so that you may marvel and be full of wonder and astonishment (John 5:19-20).

Jesus was not only going to reveal the Father and His Kingdom to the people in a greater demonstration of the works of God, but also said that we would as well.

I assure you, most solemnly I tell you, if anyone steadfastly believes in Me, he will himself be able to do the things that I do; and he will do even greater things than these, because I go to the Father (John 14:12).

Jesus and the Father are one, and the Father is also our Father. Just as He showed Jesus all things, He wants to show us all things as well. It is unto us to know the mysteries of the Kingdom. We will do greater works because we will see greater things. We need to be asking God to show us greater things and then believe, decree, and step into them by faith expecting to see His Kingdom come, His Spirit move, and His word come alive and be revealed.

Call to Me and I will answer you and show you great and mighty things, fenced in and hidden, which you do not know (do not distinguish and recognize, have knowledge of and understand) (Jeremiah 33:3).

Often times before I minister or share with churches, schools, businesses, or governments, I will privately worship and pray until this glorious rest comes upon me and I can't stand in His presence anymore. At these times, Jesus or His angels will often visit me in the realm of the Spirit and the cloud of glory. I will commune with God as a friend knows a friend and He will begin to show me heavenly things. While in the Spirit realm with God, there is an absolute assurance and knowing of faith that comes with what He is sharing. He'll then have me witness to others about what He has shared with me. There are usually tremendous signs and wonders from Heaven that endorse the revelation that is to be shared as the Kingdom of God comes in power. Afterward, I give God all of the glory and thank Him that He let me see great things by His Spirit and that He has allowed me to be His son and be in His family. Let me share some examples.

One Sunday morning while sitting on my couch and spending time with God, the weight of God's glory came upon me and I fell into a trance. The heavens opened in front of me and Jesus walked into my living room and up to the couch where I was sitting. In this experience and encounter with God, the supernatural realm and the natural realm were superimposed, one over the other.

The Lord began to share with me about His unconditional love for His bride. He asked me, "How do people get saved?" I shared, "By believing in their hearts and confessing by faith with their mouths that You are their Lord, and by repenting and turning from their sin." He said that this was true, but it started by Him first loving them. It is because God so loved the world that He sent His only begotten Son (see John 3:16). God first loved us.

The Lord Jesus asked me the same question about salvation in regards to people in almost every denomination. He would ask, "Jason, how did the Baptist get saved? How did the Anglican get saved? How did the Catholic get saved? How did the Lutheran get saved? How did the Pentecostal get saved? How did the Methodist get saved?"

After the Lord asked me the same question about almost every denomination of the church, He then asked me, "Where is everyone seated whom I called to be in My Kingdom by first loving them?"

I responded by saying, "They are seated in heavenly places in Christ" (see Eph. 2:6).

He said, "That is correct."

The Lord began to teach me how we already had unity and how it was something that was in the Spirit in Christ in heavenly places.

Then the Lord began to share with me how the whole Body of Christ is connected and one in heavenly places. When we sit together as one Body and talk bad about another denomination or person that we don't perceive to be a part of our Body, then we discern the Lord's Body wrongly. What we actually do in our pride and ignorance is hurt the corporate Body of Christ and hurt ourselves. It is as if you are taking a knife to yourself and cutting your own body. When we partner with the accuser of the brethren against God's Body that He purchased with the price of His own blood, we are in high treason against the government of God because we are now cursing what He has blessed, and speaking curses over our own lives. These curses in turn give the enemy a right of access to steal, kill, and destroy us.

This is what the apostle Paul is talking about in First Corinthians 11:27-30, and is the main reason that the Church is weak, sick, and people die prematurely. We need to be very careful what we say with our mouth and with the attitude of our heart toward Jesus' bride. Of all the people's wives in the world you don't want to talk bad about, you don't want to talk bad about Jesus' wife. It is OK to have an opinion and a voice, but make sure you have a heart of love and honor for the Church, knowing Jesus died for her and that He loves her unconditionally. He thinks she is altogether lovely and speaks to her from this place; we should do the same.

Another time while worshiping Jesus and resting in His glory I had an amazing encounter. While lying down I shared with God how much I loved Him and how thankful I was to have His presence surrounding me and in me. I was gently and lightly in rest sharing to God how special He was to me and how I loved our friendship and was so thankful for it. The presence of God continued to increase and the Holy Spirit began to flood my heart with light until the Spirit of God within my Spirit began to rise up. My eyes and ears began to open and I began to see in the realm of the Spirit and go into visions and revelations of God.

The Lord picked me up and, as I let go, I began to fly in the Spirit at incredible speeds above the freeway going south. The Lord took me to a neighborhood home outside the bottom floor. I was then lifted by the Spirit up to the second floor and went through the window into a bedroom. It was a child's bedroom. I could hear a family having dinner together downstairs and passing food around and talking.

I asked the Lord Jesus, "What am I doing here and whose house am I at?"

The Lord said to me, "This is a child's room [the name of the child was given as well], and this child has been having night-mares and tormenting demonic encounters because of the demonic activity connected to his stuffed animals that are cursed." The Lord instructed me to walk over to the closet and open the doors. When I did, there were stuffed animals on the floor inside of the closet that had demonic shadowy figures around them. These demons could see me in the realm of the Spirit, and they were aware that I could see them. They started to speak profanity and tried to intimidate me by fear.

Jesus said to me, "Jason, apply my blood as a priest and break the curse of witchcraft and the spiritual connection to these stuffed animals." I did as the Lord instructed me, and then I commanded the demons to leave this child's room as they had no legal right to be there now. They yelled and screamed, speaking rubbish, and then left. The spiritual atmosphere in the room was then filled with the Holy Spirit's presence.

After this happened, the Lord took me back to where I was praying in less than a second. I went to minister later at a church and the Lord had me share the revelation and encounter with the child's name and the location of the home. A lady stood up and shared that that was her child. The lady was also so grate-ful knowing God loves her, knows all things, and He hears and answers her prayers.

On another occasion I was in North Carolina and preparing to speak at a local church service that was held in the gymnasium of a high school. It was Easter and I was excited because to me this means His resurrection. The worship was wonderful as many people poured out their hearts of love and affection to Jesus. As I worshiped with all of my heart and all that was in me, bringing to

God a sacrifice, I became empty. As I drew near to God, He drew near to me as He promised in His Word (see James 4:8).

The presence of God began to weigh so heavy upon me that I had to lie down. The presence of His glory continued to increase until I was in complete rest and getting filled to overflowing with His love by the Holy Spirit. In this place of complete safety and security in the Father, God began to open up the heavens, and my spirit was fully activated to see, hear, and experience God and His Kingdom without the interference of the Spirit realm or atmosphere of this world. The limitations of the flesh were gone, and God began to speak to my spirit and share His heart of love for me as a person and child of His.

While receiving revelation from God and listening to His voice, a circular hole, known as a portal, opened up all around me and connected the earth with Heaven, this temporal realm with the realm of eternity. His Kingdom had come and had manifested all around me in the realm of the Spirit. Then someone in the realm of the Spirit walked over to me and stood next to me. When they stood next to me, my whole being began to coarse with warm heat, like fire, and waves of electricity flowed through every cell of my being.

I turned to see who this most profound and extraordinary presence was standing to my left. I first saw His feet, then His gown, and eventually His chest and shining, radiant face. It was the Lord Jesus!

Jesus began to speak to me about what He wanted to do in the service that morning and that He had heard the prayers of the people. He then said, "I want to show you some things about the people here and what they have prayed to me about. Then I want you to get up and share this revelation, and as you share this revelation of My Word, I'm going to answer their prayers." He also showed me that angels would be standing next to me to carry out His Word that was coming through my mouth as I released His will to be done. The angels would then do the will of God and perform His work with great exploits. This means that I wouldn't need to physically go and lay hands on any of the people, but I would only need to speak His word and He would send forth His word to heal them.

I saw a group of three angels who were there as instructed by the Lord. They were there to accompany His Word with strength to fulfill it, so His Kingdom could come and be made manifest on earth as it is in Heaven.

The Lord told me to come along with Him as He wanted to show me what some of the people prayed for and what I was to go up and call out and share afterward. I physically lay on the ground, but my spirit-man was fully activated and awake. We know God in the Spirit as He is Spirit. He outstretched His hand toward me and pulled me up. I stood up in the realm of the Spirit and watched as my natural body lay beneath me. The Lord Jesus then walked me around the room in the spirit. Both the physical and the spiritual were now one with no middle walls of separation. I could see into Heaven and earth clearly.

The Lord Jesus walked me to the right front row and showed me someone and began to tell me information about who they were and the condition they had. He then took me to the back of the right side of the room and did the same thing with another person, sharing with me who they were, what their condition was, and what they had prayed. All together the Lord took me to four different people and then walked me back up to where my body was laying. We walked right past the angels that were there to perform His word and will and stood ready on their assignment to serve Jesus.

Jesus then said to me, "When they ask you to come up and speak today, I want you to say hello and greet the people. Then I want you to begin right away and tell them what I showed and shared with you. Then I want you to pray that I would outstretch my hand to heal, set the people free, answer their prayers, and for the angels to be released to perform God's will." He shared with me that this revelation, and the ensuing miracles and wondrous signs, would open up the meeting for the people to know that God and His kingdom were present. I would then be able to minister in faith the grace of God to everyone as the Lord would lead.

I was asked to come up to minister and I greeted all of the people. I then moved into doing the will of God that I was shown by Jesus. I pointed to the four different areas of the room and started giving detailed knowledge of the people and their conditions. Every one of the people confirmed the revelation and they were in awe as there was no natural way for me to know what I did.

I continued to proceed and do the rest of what God had shown me on how to administer His kingdom. Like Moses in the wilderness, I spoke to the situation instead of physically touching them. God's angels accompanied His word through my mouth and carried out the will of God. God works all things according to the counsel of His will. The kingdom of God came upon all four people and each one received a miracle and confirming sign.

The room was now wide open, and people were in awe and expectant as God demonstrated that He is alive and present in their midst. Many more miracles began to happen as people were praying for one another. As testimonies were reported by those who received miracles, people became really excited.

The Holy Spirit shared with me that there was a gentleman with one leg shorter than the other and that God wanted to heal him by doing a creative miracle and growing His leg out. I called out the gentleman and he came up. He was a younger man, and as we prayed in front of everyone, His leg was extended inches by the creative, wonder-working power of Jesus.

Because of what happened, another man, who was very polished and sophisticated, came forward. He also had one leg shorter than the other and wanted prayer to be made whole like this younger man. I had the younger man (instead of me) pray for the older man the same way I had prayed for him. It is the Father, in Jesus' name and by His Holy Spirit, that works the miracles, and we as God's children get to work with Him. As this young man prayed for the older gentleman, the older gentleman's leg grew out as well.

The place was electric because of all of the miracles and wonders of God as God was pouring out His Spirit and revealing His glory and goodness. After I demonstrated the Gospel by the power of the Spirit, I shared about the cross, the blood of Jesus, and His death, burial, and resurrection. Numerous people got saved including the younger man whose leg had grown out!

In the realm of the Kingdom, which we have access to by God's Spirit through Jesus' blood, we can access our inheritance of heavenly treasure, wisdom, and revelation. First John 2:27 says that the anointing will teach you all things, and Jesus shared that it is given to us to know the mysteries of the Kingdom.

While in prayer, God put a desire in my heart to understand His Spirit's ways of moving from the Kingdom of God into the kingdom of earth. The Lord gave me the desire of my heart and a whole lot more. A disciple is a learner, and I am learning more and more each day.

Another time when the promised rest of God came and the eyes of my understanding were opened, I began to see into Heaven. God then took me into a room in heavenly places that was a library. In this library, books lined the walls everywhere. I was so excited to be here and wasn't sure what was permissible. I asked the Lord, "Can I read a book?"

He said, "Yes, you may."

I went and grabbed a book off of one of the book shelves. The book had PHYSICS written on its cover. As I started to open the book and read what was written on the pages, the pages came alive. The words started coming off of the pages as waves of light. The book and its content were alive! The light then began to form a scene that I went into. As I went into this scene, I could see how different dimensions worked and how God was in them all. I also saw many diagrams and illustrations that helped me to understand how the Spirit works from heaven to earth through the human spirit to manifest Christ and His works from the supernatural to the natural realm, from one plane and dimension to another.

This was one of the most amazing times with God of learning heavenly things. The wisdom, revelation, and knowledge of the glory was etched on my mind when I came out of the encounter. I soon began to partner with the Holy Spirit out of the new understanding I had. When I did, there was a whole new dimension of spiritual life and activity that opened up in and around me that was beyond the gifts of the Holy Spirit. Higher levels of realms and dimensions of reality and truth were understood, shared, and demonstrated. I always made sure I gave God all of the glory and made sure the people present would as well. This was not only my inheritance, but theirs also. God was just working through one of His sons to show what was available for all in His family and bride.

The Lord told me to go and study physics at the local bookstore. Although I loved science, I was always intimidated by physics and never took a physics class. I decided to face my fears and obey the voice of the Lord. As I approached the physics section in the bookstore, I began to feel excited in my spirit and did not know why. I started pulling books off the bookshelf to read. To my amazement, I recognized a large portion of the diagrams and illustrations used by Albert Einstein and Nicolai Tesla to explain their concepts. I had drawn these same diagrams and illustrations in my journals from my encounters with God. Although I didn't know the mathematical formulas, I understood what they were trying to communicate about space-time, gravity, light speed, vibrations, frequencies, and resonance. This was mind-blowing and awe-inspiring.

These amazing scientists saw something in their mind that, up until recently, others haven't understood. All who are in the kingdom can understand these things and more. It is our privilege. Jesus wants us to understand His thoughts and ways so we can bring His kingdom on earth as it is in Heaven.

God has since brought me into relationships with scientists, inventors, and professors from such accredited places as MIT, Harvard, and Yale. It is fascinating learning and sharing together about quantum physics and mechanics, the universe, and hyper dimensions. They are always intrigued that I have never taken a physics class and that I learned these things in Heaven by Jesus. It has turned into an amazing evangelism tool.

It has also blessed many scientists and inventors to know God gave them the desires in their heart and that He wants a personal relationship with them.

I love teaching on light, portals, and hyper dimensions because God taught me how they function and how this understanding can encourage people to grow in the knowledge of God. God's Kingdom comes in power as He demonstrates the teaching with signs and wonders over heaven and earth. As a result, people's hearts are turned to Jesus. God speaks to us in many different ways to show His desire to know each of us intimately. All knowledge and wisdom of Heaven and earth belong to the Lord, but above all, Jesus desires a heart-to-heart and Spirit-to-spirit relationship with every person.

My prayer for you is that you would fall more and more in love with Jesus and grow in love for all mankind. As we grow in love and friendship with God, He will teach us His ways and the mysteries of His Kingdom. Once we learn from God new things as His disciples, we have to apply those to our life and change our ways. May God richly bless you with a deep and intimate relationship with Him, and may you enter the promised rest of the Lord where you can hear His voice and see into His kingdom.

MORE ABOUT
AUTHOR JASON WESTERFIELD

Jason T. Westerfield is an equipper and spiritual father in the Body of Christ and is known for his love, integrity, and intimacy with God. He has a global apostolic ministry that has been accompanied by documented signs and wonders over Heaven and earth. Jason is sought out for counsel and growth development by leadership in government, business, science, media, education, and the Church. His purpose is to see God glorified and create healthy environments for families and individuals to live and work in. Jason and his wife Jessica live in the state of Connecticut in the Unites States of America with their three children: Ocean Alexander, Bella Noelle, and Justice Solomon.

5

ASCENDING INTO THE SUPERNATURAL

By Katie Souza

For years I focused on being able to hear God's voice accurately. Over a decade ago, I was sent to federal prison to serve a 13-year sentence. During my stay, I daily pressed into developing a relationship with the Lord, reading His word, worshiping, praying, and listening for Him to speak. Oh and speak He did, guiding me with His voice to receive miracles, signs, and wonders right in the middle of my imprisonment!

During that time, I learned a lot about how God speaks. I experienced many triumphs but I also made many mistakes. There were times when I thought I heard from God but I got it wrong. Other times I hit the mark. As I searched the Scriptures for the key to consistency, I found that Jesus only did what He saw the Father doing, which meant I would never fail if I did the same. Everything I touched would prosper because I would be doing the perfect will of God. (See John 14:9-13.)

As I deepened in my relationship with the Lord, He taught me many ways I could position myself to hear and see what the Father was doing. One of the most enlightening things I ever learned was how to ascend into the heavenly realms to receive wisdom directly from God. James says, *Such "wisdom" does not come down from heaven but is earthly, unspiritual, of the devil... But the wisdom that comes from heaven is first of all pure; then peace-loving, considerate, submissive, full of mercy and good fruit, impartial and sincere"* (James 3:15,17 NIV).

According to James, the wisdom that comes from this terrestrial realm is *"earthly."* What does that mean? When we seek to hear God's voice while physically standing here on this earth, a lot of things can get in the way. The word *earthly* in the *Thayer's Lexicon* speaks of the physical body we live in. We are three-part beings: body, soul, and spirit. When you are born again in Christ Jesus, your spirit man is made instantly perfect. The Bible says that the same Spirit that dwells in Christ dwells in us. Now remember Jesus only did what He saw the Father doing. So the Spirit of Christ living in you has no problem hearing the voice of God.

Your spirit may be perfected upon your born-again experience, but your soul is not. This is why we have a problem hearing the voice of God because we live in this *"earthly"* body. Our spirit lives in the tent of our flesh and our soul. Unfortunately for us, this is the place that the sin nature dwells. In Romans 7:20, 22-23 the apostle Paul said,

> *Now if I do what I do not desire to do, it is no longer I doing it [it is not myself that acts],* **but the sin [principle] which dwells within me [fixed**

and operating in my soul]....For I endorse and delight in the Law of God in my inmost self [with my new nature]. But I discern in my bodily members [in the sensitive appetites and wills of the flesh] a different law (rule of action)...making me a prisoner to the law of sin that dwells in my bodily organs [in the sensitive appetites and wills of the flesh].

Sin dwells in your *"earthly"* tent. This is why we have a hard time discerning the things of the Spirit. The signals coming from the invisible realm have to go through the filter of our corrupt soul and flesh.

Because sin dwells in us, demonic powers also have the legal right to interfere with our ability to clearly hear from God because sin provides an open door for the enemy to block or twist Heaven's revelation.

Remember what James 3:15 said, *"Such 'wisdom' does not come down from heaven but is earthly, unspiritual, **of the devil"*** (NIV). The sin residing in us gives the demonic realm legal right to harass us. That harassment can manifest in difficulty and confusion while trying to receive direction from God. Just as God wants to speak to us, so do demons! They want to plant their ideas in our minds in an effort to cause us to follow after their voice instead of the voice of the Father.

As long as our perfected spirit is confined in this earthly tent, we can be subject to these things. However, what would happen if our spirit could rise above these hindrances into the heavenly realms every time we needed direction from God? Listen again to the rest of James chapter 3.

But the wisdom that comes from heaven is first of all pure; then peace-loving, considerate, submissive, full of mercy and good fruit, impartial and sincere (James 3:17 NIV).

The wisdom from Heaven is pure and undefiled. It is untouched by sin. It is not twisted by our flesh or our soul. It is not subject to demonic influence. It is not limited to our own understanding. Heaven contains God's unlimited perfect revelation.

When seeking direction from God, we need to get up off of this earthly plane and out of our earthly tent. We need to ascend into the heavens where God's perfect answer to every problem is located. Is that Biblical? Can our spirits ascend into Heaven to get the mysteries and secrets of God, or are we bound to this earthly plane until we die?

Well, the Scripture says that we are citizens of Heaven. Philippians 3:20 states, *"But our citizenship is in heaven..."* What does that mean? A citizen is an inhabitant of a city or town, a person entitled to its privileges or franchises. Heaven is our native land. Since we are citizens of Heaven this means we have the right to have everything that is in Heaven.

What's in Heaven? Everything! The presence of God. His wisdom and revelation for any problem. Healing for any disease. Provisions for your every need. All those things, and more, are in Heaven, and because we are citizens of Heaven, it all belongs to us!

That is great news, but I always wondered how to get the stuff that is in Heaven down here to earth. Well, one way is through the supernatural tool of ascending. The word *ascend* means "to climb, or go upward, **to proceed from an inferior to a superior**

degree, to go toward the source."[1] Your source is Heaven. Every answer you need for every problem is there, but you are here on earth right now. In order for you to get up there, where all your provisions are, you need to ascend. You need to climb from this inferior plane up to that superior one. Why do I call this realm of earth the inferior plane? Hebrews 11:3 says that what is seen in this realm was made out of the invisible realm. According to Scripture, our home in Heaven is superior to what we see here. It is our source, where everything we need is contained.

Because we are citizens of Heaven, it means that we can go there anytime we want. The Bible says we have the legal right to do so. Ephesians 2:6 says, *"And God raised us up with Christ and seated us with him in the heavenly realms in Christ Jesus"* (NIV). The word *seated* means "the right of admittance to such a space." The work Jesus did on the cross won for us the legal right to be admitted into the heavens. Because of Christ, we can visit our homeland anytime we want.

How does that work? Your spirit man lives inside of you. If it were to leave, you would die because your spirit is your breath of life. However, in the eternal glory realm of Heaven, there is no time or distance. So, your spirit man can be in you and be seated in the heavenly throne room **at the same time.** That is how Ephesians 2:6 can say that you are already seated in Heaven even though you are still here on earth. Once we can really fathom this mystery, then we can really take hold of everything that is already ours by ascending into Heaven to get it.

Remember, this is one of the main things the tool of ascending can be used for—to bring all the things of Heaven to earth. The Bible actually proves this. Listen to the story in Genesis where Jacob experienced an open Heaven.

And he dreamed that there was a ladder set up on the earth, and the top of it reached to heaven; and the angels of God were ascending and descending on it! (Genesis 28:12)

There above it stood the Lord, and he said:

...I am the lord, *the God of your father Abraham and the God of Isaac; I will give you and your descendants the land on which you are lying. Your descendants will be like the dust of the earth, and you will spread out to the west and to the east, to the north and to the south. All peoples on earth will be blessed through you and your offspring. I am with you and will watch over you wherever you go, and I will bring you back to this land. I will not leave you until I have done what I have promised you* (Genesis 28:13-15 NIV).

In this story, Jacob sees Heaven open up and a ladder come down to earth. Jacob sees angels ascending and descending on the ladder, while God is at the top of the ladder speaking promises over Jacob. Notice the order in which this Scripture talks about this angelic visitation. It says that the angels were first ascending into Heaven, then they were descending. You would think it would be the other way around. Why do you think they operated in this order?

Hebrews 1:14 says that angels are ministering spirits sent to minister to those who receive salvation. So the angels Jacob saw that day were angels that were already down here on earth ministering to Jacob. The day Jacob saw the ladder the Lord was at the top of it speaking promises over Jacob. Psalms 103:20 says that angels hearken to the voice of the Word of the Lord. When God spoke those promises over Jacob, the angels that were already down here at work did what angels do. They hearkened to the voice of the Lord. When they heard God speaking those promises, they ascended up the ladder to get the stuff in Heaven needed to make those promises come to pass; then they descended back down the ladder to release provisions here!

That is one of the main reasons why we need to ascend: so we can go up into the heavenly realms to retrieve whatever we need to cause God's promises to come to pass and then bring it back down here to earth. This includes going up to get the wisdom we need to handle any situation.

Jesus talked about angels ascending in this particular order! In John 1 Jesus said to Nathanael, *"...I assure you, most solemnly I tell you all, you shall see heaven opened, and the angels of God ascending and descending upon the Son of Man!"* (John 1:51).

There is that strange order again. The angels first ascending into Heaven then descending back down. Why? Again, the job of angels is to minister to us. When Jesus was here on earth, angels attended Him. In Matthew 4:11 it says that at the end of the 40-day fast, angels came to attend Jesus. In Luke 22, when Jesus was preparing for the crucifixion in the Garden of Gethsemane, an angel came to strengthen Him. So, according to Jesus' discussion with Nathanael, when Jesus needed supernatural help, the angels that attended Him would first ascend into Heaven to get what He needed, then descend back to earth to bring it to Him.

The Bible says that angels can ascend to Heaven on our behalf. However, can human beings also ascend? I mean, it is one thing for angels to do it, but what about us?

We as men and women can do it. Does the Bible say this? Yes! The most important example of a man ascending into Heaven is Jesus Himself. When Jesus was here on earth, He came as a man. Philippians 2 says that when Jesus came to earth He shed His divinity to take on the form of a man. He even suffered and died on the cross as a man in total obedience to God. You see, Jesus Christ had to come as a man without sin or He could not be the atoning sacrifice for the rest of humankind.

So Jesus came to earth as a man like us. In John 3, Jesus makes a statement that proves that He would ascend into His native land of Heaven while he was here on earth. Jesus was talking to Nicodemus when He said, *"I have spoken to you of earthly things and you do not believe; how then will you believe if I speak of heavenly things?* **No one has ever gone into heaven except the one who came from heaven—the Son of Man"** (John 3:12-13 NIV). In this Scripture, Jesus is talking about ascending and descending. He tells Nicodemus that although He descended from Heaven to earth, **He was also ascended in Heaven while He was on earth**. Ephesians 2:6 says that we are seated in heavenly realms. Christ was the first one to do it! While He was here, His spirit man was operating inside of Him while simultaneously being able to operate in Heaven. Jesus was setting a standard for the rest of humankind to follow.

Being able to ascend into Heaven seems a mystery too impossible for us to fathom. Jesus knew we would have difficulty understanding it at first. That is why He said to Nicodemus, *"I have spoken to you of earthly things and you do not believe; how then will you believe if I speak of heavenly things? No one has ever gone into heaven except the one who came from heaven—the Son of Man"* (John 3:12-13 NIV). The Bible says that Nicodemus was a Pharisee, a leader among the Jews and a teacher of Scripture. Yet, when Jesus shared this heavenly truth with him, he could not comprehend it.

However, just because we can't fully grasp something from Scripture doesn't negate that it is still truth. Jesus said, *"I have still many things to say to you, but you are not able to bear them or to take them upon you or to grasp them now. But when He, the Spirit of Truth (the Truth-giving Spirit) comes, He will guide you into all the Truth (the whole, full Truth)* (John 16:12-13).

In the Kingdom of Heaven, there are deep mysteries. Scripture is full of layers. As we dig into them, the Holy Spirit will reveal to us heavenly things that we could not fathom before. As we search through Scripture, we see that many men in the Bible ascended into their homeland of Heaven. In the book of Revelation, the apostle John had this experience.

> *After this I looked, and behold, a door standing open in heaven! And the first voice which I had heard addressing me like [the calling of] a war trumpet said, Come up here, and I will show you what must take place in the future. At once I came under the [Holy] Spirit's power, and behold, a throne stood in heaven, with One seated on the throne!* (Revelation 4:1-2)

John was just a man; yet, he ascended into the heavenly realm. Notice that each time someone went up into Heaven, it was so they could have an encounter with God, and so they could receive revelations. Look at all the downloads John received while he was ascended into Heaven. The entire Book of Revelation was written from His experience!

Exodus 24:9-11 is another proof of men ascending into the heavens. The Scripture says that when Israel was at the foot of mount Horab,

> *Moses and Aaron...and the seventy elders of Israel went up and saw the God of Israel. Under His feet was something like a pavement made of sapphire, clear as the sky itself...they saw God, and they ate and drank* (Exodus 24:9-11 NIV).

Moses, Aaron, and the elders of Israel ascended into the throne room of God, and they were just men. Notice that the Scripture says that they ate and drank. This tells me that more than their spirits went up into Heaven, but their bodies ascended also. Are there other Scriptures to substantiate the claim that we can go up into Heaven in more than our physical bodies?

Well, the apostle Paul said we can. Listen to this Scripture from Second Corinthians.

> *True, there is nothing to be gained by it, but [as I am obliged] to boast, I will go on to visions and revelations of the Lord. I know a man in Christ who fourteen years ago—whether in the body or out of the body I do not know, God knows—was caught up to the third heaven. And I know that this man—whether in the body or away from the*

body I do not know, God knows—was caught up into paradise, and he heard utterances beyond the power of man to put into words, which man is not permitted to utter...(2 Corinthians 12:1-4).

Paul says twice *"whether in the body or out of the body I do not know, God knows"* (2 Cor. 12:2-3 NKJV). When something is mentioned twice in Scripture, you need to pay attention to it. According to Paul, human beings can ascend into the heavenly realm both in the spirit and in our physical bodies.

Let me tell you a story. My husband and I live in a small city in the middle of the Arizona desert. There are a lot of dust storms out there. When they happen, the air gets absolutely filled with sand and dirt. If I am outside, I get a massive sinus headache from breathing in the dirt.

Well, one Sunday we were home. We just finished a conference the day before, so we were very tired. It was a nice day with a strong breeze, so we opened all the windows. We decided to rest and take a nap. As I lay down, I ascended into Heaven. As I did, I saw the strangest vision, a profile of my face and a big huge ball of nose hair sticking out my nostrils!

That's all I remember; then I was out. An hour or so later, I woke up to the curtains flapping in the wind. I opened my eyes and the whole room was totally foggy. I reached over to turn on the lamp, and as I did, I saw stuff falling off my arm and off the sheets. When I turned on the light, I realized it was dirt! A major dust storm had risen up while we were asleep. Since we left all the windows open, the air inside was totally filled with dirt and there was a layer of dirt on everything in our house!

So my husband and I jumped up, and for the next 3 hours we vacuumed, swept, and wiped down the entire house. As I was finishing up, I realized I didn't have a severe sinus headache like I normally would from breathing in the dust. I began wondering how that could be since I was breathing in dirt for hours! Right then, God brought back to me the picture I saw as I was ascending up to Heaven, the big ball of nose hair sticking out of my nostrils.

I was so intrigued; I went online to look it up. I found that the main function of nose hair is to keep foreign or unwanted particles from entering the lungs, thus damaging your respiratory system. When I read that, I got really excited. I realized that we were protected from breathing in all that massive amount of dirt that filled the air in our house when I went up to Heaven! As I was putting all this together, I ran into the bathroom, blew my nose, and looked at the Kleenex. There was not a spec of dirt in that Kleenex, which was absolutely impossible considering the dust storm and cleaning. If you have ever been outside during a dust storm, you know that dirt will always go in your nose as you are breathing in the air. But there was not one speck of dirt in mine.

Now what did Paul say? He knew a man who went up into the third heavens, whether in the body or out of the body He did not know. I felt exactly the same way. To this day, I am still not sure whether I only went up in the spirit, because my physical body was not touched by that dirt.

The Bible makes it clear that men ascended into Heaven, and they didn't do it for just a thrill ride. Every time someone went up, they had an encounter with God or they received revelation. When Moses and the elders went up, they got to see the Lord.

They got to encounter God, and eat and drink with Him. When John went up, he received Heaven's instruction to give to the seven churches. Plus, he received the download for the whole Book of Revelation. When the man whom Paul was speaking about went up, he heard utterances that were too powerful to put into words, revelation that humankind was not permitted to speak.

We should not look at ascending as some kind of a flighty supernatural high. Ascending is a tool that God has given to help us bring the things of the Kingdom of Heaven here to earth. This includes the wisdom of Heaven that can enable us to solve any problem.

I was on tour in Oklahoma. When I arrived, I could sense there was something going on in the spirit. So instead of trying to use my own reasoning to figure it out, I asked the Lord to take me up. When He took me, I saw a vision of two witches in black hats and caps with their backs to me. They didn't know I was there. One was sitting at the east, the other at the west. When I came out of the vision I asked God what was up with them. I heard Him say, "They travel together."

When I asked our host what she knew about two witches that traveled together, she said the largest witchcraft covens in that state were in that county. She said those covens didn't stay in one place, but they would travel from east to west. When I asked God what to do about it, He said one word to me: *elevate*. Right then, I knew He wanted me to ascend.

When I did ascend, I found my spirit man flying through the sky, looking down at a witch who was flying west on a broom. I was above her, so I just saw the back of her head and her back. She was not aware I was there. I saw this for just a few seconds; then, I just commanded her to fall in the name of Jesus. Immediately, she began tumbling out of the sky down to the ground. Then, the same thing happened again. All of a sudden, I was over a witch that was flying east. Again, I commanded her to fall in the name of Jesus. She also tumbled out of the sky to the earth. That week, signs and wonders took place in that area! The people in that county had prayed for years against those covens. Through the tool of ascending, they were defeated in 20 minutes! When you learn how to ascend, the battle against the enemy will be fast and decisive.

Now I am going to give you some simple steps that will help position you to ascend.

If you really want to be able to ascend easily all the time, one of the best things you can do is cultivate an open heaven in your home. What do I mean by that? In Heaven there are doors, windows, and gates that, when opened, allow you access to Heaven so you can easily ascend and descend. Remember what Jesus said in John 1 "*...I assure you, most solemnly I tell you all, you shall see **heaven opened**, and the angels of God ascending and descending upon the Son of Man!*" (John 1:51). You see, the heavens were opened first; then the angels began to ascend. When the apostle John got taken up to Heaven he said, "*Behold a **door standing open** in heaven*" (Rev. 4:1 NKJV). John so easily ascended into Heaven because there was first an open door.

One simple way to get those doors to open is with your thanksgiving and praise. Psalms 100 says that we "*enter into His gates with thanksgiving, and into His courts with praise*" (Ps. 100:4 NKJV). When you cultivate a flow of praise, thanksgiving, and worship in your home, it literally opens the heavens. One of the greatest things you can do is spend time every day in focused worship. I carve out daily time to fiercely focus on the Lord. I mean **fiercely** focus. If my mind gets distracted, I bring it back to the Lord immediately. Scripture says that we need to offer a sacrifice of praise. If you will take time to do this, you will carve out an open heaven in your home. This will enable the things of Heaven to flow down into your home and enable you to easily ascend up into the heavens.

The next step that enables you to ascend into the heavens is to wash in the blood of Jesus Christ. Remember Ephesians 2:6 says that we are seated in heavenly realms with Christ. Now listen to the verse that is right before it. Ephesians 2:5 says, *"Even when we were dead in sins, [He] hath quickened us together with Christ, (by grace ye are saved)"* (KJV). You have the right to go into Heaven **because** you are being cleansed of your sin by the atoning work Jesus did on the cross.

We need to be washed of our sin before we ascend the mountain of God. Let me give you an Old Testament example. In Exodus 19, the Israelite people were at the foot of Mount Horab. God called to Moses and told him to sanctify the Israelites because He was going to come down on the mountain to visit the people. As part of God's instructions to prepare the people for this visitation, the Lord told Moses this, *"And you shall **set bounds for the people round about**, saying, Take heed that you go not up into the mountain or touch the border of it. Whoever touches the mountain shall surely be put to death...The Lord said to Moses, **Go down and warn the people, lest they break through to the Lord to gaze and many of them perish** (Exod. 19:12, 21 AMP).*

The people were so anxious to see the Lord that barriers were erected at the base of the mountain to hold them back, and the people were warned not to cross over them. Why were barriers erected? Because the law, which would enable the people to be washed of their sins, had not been given yet. So if the people ascended up the mountain with their sin all over them, they would perish in the presence of the holiness of God!

After Moses built the barriers that sanctified the people, God came down in all His glory to verbally speak the commandments to the Israelites. Afterward, the Scripture says this,

> *When the people saw the thunder and lightning and heard the trumpet and saw the mountain in smoke, they trembled with fear. They stayed at a distance and said to Moses, "Speak to us yourself and we will listen. But do not have God speak to us or we will die." Moses said to the people,* **"Do not be afraid. God has come to test you, so that the fear of God will be with you to keep you from sinning." The people remained at a distance, while Moses approached the thick darkness where God was** (Exodus 20:18-21 NIV).

Do you hear that? The people didn't want to hear the law from God. They couldn't receive it. Moses responded to them by saying **"Do not be afraid. God has come to test you, so that the fear of God will be with you to keep you from sinning"** (Exod. 20:20 NIV). Moses understood that their sin was keeping them from ascending up the mountain to be with the Lord. Moses knew that if they didn't receive His commandments and get washed from their sins that separation would continue.

Now listen to what the very next verse says, **"The people remained at a distance, while Moses approached the thick darkness where God was"** (Exod. 20:21 NIV). The people were cut off from a supernatural encounter with God because of their sin while Moses, who understood the importance of holiness, ascended into God's presence.

I would advise you to be washed in the blood before you meet with God. If you do this, you will find the barrier which has been erected at the bottom of the mountain will be removed; then you will easily ascend into the presence of God like Moses did.

Now, once you wash, spend some time praying in tongues. Jude 1:20 says, *"But you, beloved, build yourselves up [founded] on your most holy faith [make progress, **rise like an edifice higher and higher**], praying in the Holy Spirit"*. As you pray in the Spirit, you will build yourself up; then your spirit man will rise higher and higher toward the heavens. Sometimes I will pray this way for an hour before I try to ascend, especially if I am having a difficult time going up.

Once you wash, then pray in the spirit and you're ready to go up. You can start by making a decree that you have the right to do so. Job 22:28 says, *"You shall also decide and **decree** a **thing**, and it shall be established for you; and the light [of God's favor] shall shine upon your ways."* Before you go up, decree you have the right to go up. You can also decree Philippians 3:20 and Ephesians 2:6 out loud. Remember, you are a citizen of Heaven and you are seated in heavenly realms with Christ. As you are speaking these Scriptures, it will establish your biblical right to ascend into the heavenlies.

Now, as you begin to ascend, you will need to activate your faith. The Bible says that we are able to ascend into the heavens by faith. In Hebrews 11:5 it says,

> *Because of faith Enoch was caught up and trans-*
> *ferred to heaven, so that he did not have a glimpse*
> *of death; and he was not found, because God had*

translated him. For even before he was taken to heaven, he received testimony [still on record] that he had pleased and been satisfactory to God .

The Scriptures say that without faith it is not possible to please God (see Heb. 11:6). Obviously, Enoch was a man who pleased God because of his faith—so much so that it was his faith which enabled him to ascend into Heaven without first experiencing death.

What else should you do to get ready to go up? You need to know that the Spirit of God living in you will enable you to ascend. When the apostle John ascended into Heaven, a voice said to him,

...Come up here, and I will show you what must take place in the future. ***At once I came under the [Holy] Spirit's power,*** *and behold, a throne stood in heaven, with One seated on the throne!* (Revelation 4:1-2)

It was through the power of the Spirit that John was able to ascend.

Another point is this. You can command your spirit to go up. John's spirit received a command to come up to Heaven. The Bible says you can ascend because of Christ's work on the cross. It will not be out of line for you to command your spirit man to go up just like John's spirit was commanded.

One way you can position your self physically to go up is to let yourself go into a deep sleep, or what the Bible calls a trance. When I do this, I get really clear visions and hear very clearly. The word *trance* means "a half-conscious state, seemingly between sleeping and waking, in which ability to function voluntarily may be suspended."

In Acts 22, the apostle Paul went into a trance. Scripture says that after Paul received his sight after being knocked of his horse, he fell into a trance. *"When I returned to Jerusalem and was praying at the temple, **I fell into a trance and saw the Lord speaking**"* (Acts 22:17-18 NIV). Paul went into a trance, a half-conscious state, seemingly between sleeping and waking. During the trance, he saw a very clear vision of the Lord speaking instruction to him. When you allow yourself to be pulled into a trance-like state, it will allow you to see very clearly in the spirit.

In Acts 10 it says that Peter went into a trance. Listen to what happened.

> *The next day as they were still on their way and were approaching the town, Peter went up to the roof of the house to pray, about the sixth hour (noon). But he became very hungry, and wanted something to eat; and while the meal was being prepared a trance came over him, and he saw the sky opened and something like a great sheet lowered by the four corners, descending to the earth. It contained all kinds of quadrupeds and wild beasts and creeping things of the earth and birds of the air. And there came a voice to him, saying, Rise up, Peter, kill and eat. But Peter said, No, by no means, Lord; for I have never eaten anything that is common and unhallowed or [ceremonially] unclean. And the voice came to him again a second time, What God has cleansed and*

pronounced clean, do not you defile and profane by regarding and calling common and unhallowed or unclean. This occurred three times; then immediately the sheet was taken up to heaven (Acts 10:9-16).

Notice that when Peter was in that trance, he saw visions from Heaven, and he heard the voice of the Lord very clearly. When we are in a deep sleep or a trance-like state, our spirits can go up easily and we can see and hear things clearly.

You will know if you are going into a trance because you will feel a heaviness come over you, a strong pull to go to sleep. If you feel that coming on you while you ascend, don't fight it. Take your pillow and lie down.

I like to get up an hour earlier then I normally do so I am still sleepy. I pray in tongues until my mind gets quiet. Then I lie back down and allow myself to go into that deep sleep. I keep my journal next to me so when I start seeing or hearing things, I wake myself up and write it down.

That brings me to my next point. Interact with whatever you see in Heaven. If God takes you up then shows you a friend who is sick, command that individual to become well. If God shows you sin, then put the blood of Jesus on it. If He shows you something that you don't understand, ask Him what it means.

Now before you descend, ask the Lord what He wants you to bring back. Whatever He tells you, grab hold of it by faith, and bring it back. Anything you see in these encounters is yours because the Bible says in Deuteronomy,

*The secret things belong unto the Lord our God, but the **things which are revealed belong to us and to our children forever**, that we may do all of the words of this law* (Deuteronomy 29:29).

A few years ago, during the famine that hit America, my husband's company closed down. They only booked one job in a year's time. His unemployment ran out, and we were in trouble. Instead of trying to figure out what to do on our own, I asked the Lord to take me up to Heaven so I could get God's wisdom from above. While there, I saw my husband walk over to a safe, open it up, and take out a big diamond. I asked the Lord what I should do with it. He said, "The things revealed to you belong to you." So, by faith, I took that diamond back with me to earth and released it. A week later, my husband got a job worth a quarter of a million dollars!

ENDNOTE

1. *Random House Unabridged Dictionary,* Copyright © 1997, by Random House, Inc.

MORE ABOUT
AUTHOR KATIE SOUZA

KATIE SOUZA is the founder and president of Expected End Ministries. She has been featured on TBN, 700 Club, God TV, Extreme Prophetic, Sid Roth, and numerous radio shows in the United States. Her powerful testimony of turning captivity into promise has changed the lives of many people around the globe. She is the author of "The Captivity Series: The Key To Your Expected End" which is currently being taught in over 500 prisons around the world. In this season, she is furiously pursuing the light of Jesus to heal the souls of believers everywhere. Come join her in her pursuit and your life will forever be transformed.

For more information on ascending, get my teaching called *"Ascending Into the Supernatural."* Also, if you want to get your soul healed so you can really go up fast, get *"The Glory Light of Jesus Heals Your Soul."*

6

HEARING AIDS

By Kevin Dedmon

I met Theresa about a year after becoming a Christian. I was 18 and in love. Our first date was dinner and street witnessing, in which we led five people to the Lord and held hands for the first time! At that moment, we knew that we wanted to pursue marriage.

After a year of dating, however, we discovered differences in our personalities and temperaments, upbringings, and educational backgrounds that could make for a challenging course for marriage. We were told that these differences would not allow for a long and happy marriage, so we decided to break off the relationship. In addition, we felt that it would be best to completely sever all communication, so that it would be easier to get on with the good purposes that God had for each one of us—the idea being that the passion we felt for each other would dissipate as soon as we were separated.

After only one day, however, I was miserable. Furthermore, by the end of the first week, all I could think of was Theresa. I continually prayed that the love I had for her would vanish, but instead, it just increased all the more. The next week, I even tried to hate her, thinking that doing so would change my desire to still want to be with her, but I could not think of one thing that I did not like about her. Ironically, I found that my love for her was growing daily!

I was in a dilemma. In my head, I truly wanted God's will for our lives because I believed separating provided us with the greatest possibility of fulfilling our destiny, leading to true happiness. Furthermore, I believed God had someone perfect for me as well, and I was willing to wait until she came along. In my heart, however, I truly did not want to spend the rest of my life without Theresa. I was miserable without her in my life. I did not want anyone else! She was my perfect one, even with all of the potential challenges!

The problem was that Theresa had resolved the same course of action as I had, so much so, that she went to a secluded cabin to seek God's direction for her new life without me. She was gone. Our relationship was over.

I so wanted to call her in order to tell her of my feelings, and the mistake we had made in calling off our engagement, but the cabin where she was staying had no phone (this was a time before cell phones). After that second week, I could not take the pain of my dilemma any longer—I needed to hear a clear word from God about His will for my life.

Having been a Christian only a few years, and having just read through the Bible one rudimentary time, I somehow remembered that Gideon had asked God for a sign to let him know what he was to do with regards to leading Israel into battle against the Midianites (see Judg. 6-7).

In that instance, he laid out a fleece (probably an article of clothing made of wool), and asked the Lord to answer his specific request. The first night, he asked that God would cause the wool to be covered with dew, but leave the ground dry. Of course, after God answered that request, Gideon asked Him to reverse the request—that the ground would be wet, and the fleece dry. The answer to that specific request gave Gideon the confidence to take on the mighty Midianite army and defeat them with only 300 men!

So I decided to take Gideon's example, and lay down a fleece regarding my destiny with Theresa. In my desperation to hear from God, I decided to make an impossible demand, asking for the fulfillment of a specific sign that would clearly speak His will for my future with Theresa.

At that time, I had not spoken with Theresa for two weeks, and as far as I knew, she was already pursuing a new life without me. My fleece was that she would call me before I counted to one hundred. I had resolved that if she did not call, then I would never question our decision to sever our relationship again and somehow get on with my life.

I'll never forget the sinking feeling in my heart, sitting in the basement of my parents' home, as I began to count off the numbers in silence. At 80, I began to count slower, as I could not bear the reality that I would have to live the rest of my life without Theresa.

I was on 96 when the phone rang. My heart immediately stopped, and then pumped with unimaginable adrenaline, as I heard my father answering the phone upstairs, saying, "Yes, he's here. I'll get him." I don't think I even touched the steps as I bounded up to the phone.

Trying to keep my composure, I listened as Theresa explained that she had been praying over the past two weeks, and that she could not bear being apart despite the potential challenges we faced. She went on to say that she had felt an overwhelming urge to call me, even though we had agreed to sever all communication. Amazingly, she had driven to a little market a mile away during a snowstorm in order to make the call!

I could not contain myself as I shared about the fleece that I had asked God to speak through. Afterward, through rejoicing tears, we determined that God had truly spoken to both of us, and that we were destined to be together for the rest of our lives.

Six months later, we were married. Over the years, we have encountered some of the challenges that we had foreseen during our engagement, as well as some unplanned storms, but hearing the clarity of God's voice in answer to our heart's desire to know His will has motivated us to work things out each time. As a result, we have enjoyed over 30 years of blessing together—and still counting!

HONING IN ON GOD'S VOICE

I believe hearing God's voice is essential in fulfilling our destiny and experiencing God's blessing in life. Thirty-four times we find the phrase, "Hear the word of the Lord," spoken by the prophets in the Old Testament. We must be able to clearly hear God's voice in order to know God's will, as well as gain wisdom and direction for our lives.

Before Jesus entered into His public ministry, He heard His Father's voice from Heaven saying, *"This is my Son, whom I love; with him I am well pleased"* (Matt. 3:17 NIV). The timing of this encounter seems to indicate that Jesus needed to hear His Father's voice in order to be activated into His destiny as the Messiah. It was not until Jesus heard those specific words that confirmed His identity, and the love and approval of His Father, that He began to preach and perform miracles, demonstrating that the Kingdom of God was among them.

Interestingly, however, after Jesus heard those words, and before He entered into His destined Messianic ministry, He had to undergo a time of testing. Immediately after Jesus' encounter, in which He clearly heard His Father's voice, we find Him being tempted in the wilderness (see Matt. 4:1-11). Twice in this passage, the devil tested Jesus with the words, *"If you are the Son of God…."* In other words, "Did you really hear God correctly?"

Notice the questioning, *"If,"* even though the Father's words, *"This is my son,"* were clear. I believe the devil understood that if he could get Jesus to doubt His hearing, it would debilitate and prevent Him from fulfilling His destiny. Jesus' confidence in stepping into His destiny was contingent upon a clear word from His Father. Any doubt of what was said could thwart the plans and purposes of God in and through His life.

Similarly, the devil used the same tactic in the Garden of Eden when he tempted Eve asking, *"Did God really say?"* (Gen. 3:1). In other words, "Did God really mean that?" The devil's strategy was to dilute and distort the truth of what God had said, in order to divert Eve from the good plans and purposes of God—to prevent her, and subsequently Adam—from fulfilling their true destiny.

Adam and Eve were destined to exercise authority over the earth, managing what God had created (see Gen. 1:28). Instead, they were subdued by sin, resulting in bondage and death, because Eve was deceived into doubting what she had clearly heard God say. Adam and Eve lost their God-given authority to represent God's Kingdom because they succumbed to the seduction of satan's strategy to deceive them by contesting the word of the Lord.

So then, we could argue that the authority and confidence to release the Kingdom of God is founded upon the ability to hone in on the voice of God and to clearly understand the significance of what He says. Moreover, the ability to hear God's voice determines the level of risk we are willing to take to accomplish God's will in and through our lives.

Unfortunately, there are so many voices vying for our attention that it is sometimes difficult to discern God's voice amongst so many. Scientists estimate that the average person has approximately 70,000 thoughts per day.[1]

That is a lot of thinking! Obviously, not all of those thoughts are from God. Our thoughts come from many different sources trying to vie for our listening attention. There are many different voices trying to influence us—the media, other people, self, satan, as well as God, to identify just a few.

Throughout history, there are many accounts of people who have claimed to have heard from God, while, in fact, they were just manipulating and controlling others for their own selfish desires. Moreover, many people have been deceived by satan, subsequently deceiving others, while thinking they were truly hearing from God.

The quest, then, is to determine God's voice from among all of the varying voices speaking to us. Samuel worked through this process when Eli helped him discern God's voice when he was serving in the temple. As a result, he became a prophet to Israel (see 1 Sam. 3:1-18). As with Samuel, then, a key to fulfilling our destiny is the ability to hear and discern the voice of God.

The good news is that those who belong to God can hear His voice (see John 8:47). In John 10:27, Jesus promised that, *"My sheep listen to my voice..."* (NIV). In other words, we are able to discern His voice from among all of the other voices giving us direction.

In John 10:3-4, Jesus uses a figure of speech to describe the way in which believers are designed to hear from God when He says,

> *...The sheep listen to his voice. He calls his own sheep by name and leads them out. When he has brought out all his own, he goes on ahead of them, and his sheep follow him because they know his voice* (NIV).

So then, the question for us to consider is not whether or not God is speaking, but whether we can hear Him as He is speaking. I want to encourage you that you can hear God's voice clearly.

In the remainder of this chapter, I want to give you three "hearing aids" that have helped me catch God's voice. They are certainly not comprehensive of all of the aids available, but I only have one chapter.

HEARING AID #1
HUNGER

I believe Theresa was inspired to drive to that little market in a snowstorm to call me on number 96 because of my hunger to hear from God. I have had many other desperate occasions since.

Each time, in my hunger, the Lord has spoken to me in clear ways, leaving no doubt that I had heard His voice.

Webster's Dictionary defines *hunger* as "a strong desire or passion—it is a craving for something."[2] When I crave something, I go on a mission to satisfy that desire. When craving God's voice, I am relentless until I am able to clearly hear from Him.

I love the way Solomon describes the bride's desire to hear her bridegroom's voice when he writes,

> *My dove in the clefts of the rock, in the hiding places on the mountainside, show me your face, let me hear your voice; for your voice is sweet, and your face is lovely* (Song of Solomon 2:14 NIV).

Again, in Song of Solomon 8:13, the bride expresses her hunger to hear from her lover when she says, *"You who dwell in the gardens with friends in attendance, let me hear your voice!"* (NIV). This is a cry of desperation—she must hear his voice. Thus, she is completely focused.

In Proverbs 16:26, Solomon observes that, *"The laborer's appetite works for him; his hunger drives him on"* (NIV). When we are hungry to hear God's voice, our craving drives us until we are rewarded.

The writer to the Hebrews promised that, *"He* [God] *rewards those who earnestly seek Him"* (Heb. 11:6 NIV). Another translation for the phrase "earnestly seek Him" is to "crave Him." In the context of hearing God's voice, our hunger, craving to hear, is rewarded in His speaking to us.

When we hunger for God's voice, the Scriptures promise that He will give us what we crave of Him. Jesus promised, *"Blessed [hugely happy] are those who hunger and thirst for righteousness, for they will be filled"* (Matt. 5:6 NIV). He also assured that if we ask, we will receive (see Matt. 7:7; Luke 11:9).

David states that, *"He satisfies the thirsty and fills the hungry with good things"* (Ps. 107:9; see also Luke 1:53 NIV). God responds to our hunger. Our hunger to hear God's voice actually draws His voice toward us.

In Psalm 38:12-15, David expresses his hunger to hear from God in the following verses:

> *Those who seek my life set their traps, those who would harm me talk of my ruin; all day long they plot deception. I am like a deaf man, who cannot hear, like a mute, who cannot open his mouth; I have become like a man who does not hear, whose mouth can offer no reply. I wait for you, O Lord; you will answer, O Lord my God* (NIV).

I believe David's confidence is rooted in the testimony of how God has faithfully spoken to him, and others, in the past when they were desperate for His voice. Therefore, his desperation was a sign that he could count on God's answer. In the same way, when we live in a place of desperation (hunger), God is faithful to answer us.

The key, then, is to stay hungry. To that end, I try to keep myself in a place in which I need to hear from God. For example, there are times while at a restaurant that I will announce to those at my table that I am going to get some words of knowledge for our server. Often, it is when I feel the adrenaline pumping, knowing he or she is on the way to our table, that I become desperate to hear God's voice.

On one occasion, my wife and I were on a "mini-moon" get away in Lake Tahoe, California. One night, while eating at a local restaurant, I suggested that we change the atmosphere, and "blow the place up!" I told Theresa that I was going to get a word of knowledge for our server. Making that statement put a demand on my ability to hear the voice of God, which resulted in an immediate desperation for Him to speak to me.

When our server returned to our table, I heard, "bronchial problem." It turned out that she had intense allergies that were severely affecting her bronchial system. Theresa and I prayed for her, and immediately she felt better. Shocked, she explained that her lungs were completely open, and she could breathe normally. Excitedly, she also exclaimed that her headache, another symptom of the allergies, had left.

As we were leaving, I noticed a couple sitting behind us. Once again, I told Theresa that I was going to minister to them. I had not heard anything from the Lord about them, so I just stopped and said to the husband, "Excuse me, this might sound a little strange, but by any chance do you have any [and then at that moment, I heard the words] back pain?"

Interestingly, I only heard the specific words as I stepped out into a place in which I had to hear. The man responded, "How did you know that?" While holding a forkful of spaghetti, he explained how he had experienced intense pain in his back throughout dinner. As I began to release the presence of Jesus on him, his pain completely left.

Theresa and I began to get words of knowledge about the wife's inability to sleep, and how God wanted to give her peace. She began to weep, as she confirmed that she indeed had a sleep disorder, and was constantly filled with anxiety.

We shared some comforting words from Father's heart, and spoke assuring words of God's destiny for her life. Afterward, she explained that she could feel the insecurity and fear leaving. We could all see a visible peace and relief on her countenance. In the end, she expressed that she had never felt so good.

We introduced both of them to the Jesus who had just touched them, and when we left their table about ten minutes later, we were like long-time friends, all because I had put myself in a position in which I had to hear from God.

At my church, I oversee a Firestarters class—a twelve-week course designed to train newcomers and new believers in a revival lifestyle. Each week, we make our students take risks. Sometimes, without any prior notice, we have them turn to someone sitting next to them and prophesy to them. At other times, we ask for volunteers to come to the front, and make them prophesy to someone that we have picked out of the crowd. We will do the same with words of knowledge for healing.

Amazingly, our "newbie" Firestarters always hear from God, even though, prior to stepping out in risk, they had not heard a thing. There is something about being put on the spot that causes us to *hone in* on His voice.

When we put ourselves in a position in which we must hear from God, we become more desperate and attentive. Pursuing a lifestyle of risk helps us in developing hunger. If we never live on the edge, pursuing our destiny, then there is a little felt need to hear from God. Conversely, when we find ourselves living as radical revivalists, we begin to hunger and crave His voice, and that is when we will be better able to catch His voice.

HEARING AID #2
HANGING ON EVERY WORD

In Matthew 4:4, Jesus said, *"Man does not live on bread alone, but on every word that comes from the mouth of God"* (NIV). In other words, bread is important in order to sustain life, but our true life sustenance comes from ingesting and digesting the word of God. We will never be able to experience the fullness of life without hearing the voice of God.

Interestingly, the Greek word translated *word* here is not "graphe," which means "writing," and is translated "Scripture" in the New Testament. It is important to note that Jesus was not proclaiming that man should live on every *graphe*. Rather, He used the Greek word, *rhema* to describe the *word* coming from the mouth of God, which basically means "communication" or "conversation."

Vine's Expository Dictionary of New Testament Words defines *rhema* as, "a statement, command, or instruction." It refers to speech itself or a discourse whether oral or written. It is "the act and process of communication."[3] Hence, in Matthew 4, Jesus declared that it was God's intention for man to have an ongoing conversation with Him in the context of relationship—communion (communication).

In Romans 10:8, the apostle Paul encourages that, *"the word [rhema] is near you..."* (NIV). In other words, God's voice is always near enough to be heard. In Romans 10:17, Paul further explains that, *"faith comes from hearing, and hearing by the word [rhema] of Christ"* (NASB). So then, our faith comes by the conversation we have with God in the communion of His presence.

Moreover, part of our armor as Christians is *"the sword of the Spirit, which is the word [rhema] of God"* (Eph. 6:17 NIV). The way in which Jesus defeated the enemy's temptations was to hang on every word that His Father spoke. He overcame because He had a continual conversation with God the Father.

Now certainly, God speaks through the Scriptures (*graphe*). In fact, the apostle Paul points out that,

> *All Scripture is God-breathed and is useful for teaching, rebuking, correcting and training in righteousness, so that the man of God may be thoroughly equipped for every good work* (2 Timothy 3:16-17 NIV).

We have been given a miraculous gift in the Scriptures to help us hear from God.

Furthermore, God does not contradict what He has already said in Scripture, yet the Scripture is not comprehensive of all that God is speaking. Moreover, God is not fully contained within the confines of Scripture; there is more to God than what is revealed in Scripture, and there is more that He is saying in His conversation with us.

For example, the apostle Paul expresses the need for spiritual gifts when he states, *"Now I know in part; then I shall know fully, even as I am fully known"* (1 Cor. 13:12 NIV). Spiritual gifts facilitate our hearing from God apart from Scripture, although everything needs to be evaluated in the context of what God has already spoken in Scripture, as God does not contradict what He has already said (see 1 Cor. 14:29).

On the other hand, we do not need a proof text of Scripture for everything God says to us. There was nothing in the Scriptures that could speak to my destiny with Theresa. I needed to hear a personal word from God about my personal situation—I needed a personal encounter, in which I had a conversation, so to speak, with God.

Jesus made the point in John 5:39-40, when He said,

> *You diligently study the Scriptures because you think that by them you possess eternal life. These are the Scriptures that testify about me, yet you refuse to come to me to have life* (NIV).

It is important to note that Jesus was not discounting Scripture. Rather, He was putting it in proper perspective. His point was that true life comes from a relationship with God, not information about God.

Earlier in this discourse, Jesus said, *"I tell you the truth, whoever hears my word* ["*logos*" in this context can be translated "message"] *and believes Him who sent me has eternal life and will not be condemned; he has crossed over from death to life"* (John 5:24 NIV). Therefore, hearing the voice of the Lord is essential in experiencing eternal life in the future, as well as in our present daily life.

Over the years, I have met many people who have studied the Scriptures but do not have the life of God. There are people who constantly hear the Scriptures, yet they still do not have a relationship with Christ. The Scriptures are intended for us to have a *rhema* relationship with God.

In order to fully comprehend the meaning of the Greek word *rhema*, we must also grasp the underlying meaning of the Greek word *logos*. Moreover, *rhema* can only be understood in the context of *logos*.

John the apostle identifies Jesus as the *Logos*, referring to Him as the Word (*Logos*) of God (*Theos*)—the full expression and manifestation of God (see John 1:1-14). Jesus, therefore, perfectly communicates, embodies, and demonstrates the nature, character, personality, and attributes of God the Father.

The Greek word *logos* originated in Alexandrian times and simply referred to "speech, communication, or an utterance" in the classical Greek language. *Logos* also embodied the creativity, logic, ideas, and reason underlying the speech, communication, or utterance, as well as the effects of whatever was communicated.[4]

Later, in Greek philosophy, the *Logos* (the Word) was additionally defined as the full expression of God (*Theos*)—the Word of God. The Greeks, of course, believed in many gods, but the highest, most supreme "god" was the *Logos*, the Word, which empowered all of the others.

The *Logos* represented everything that God was communicating and was considered to be the supreme source of all creativity, reason, power, and will in the universe; it was the underlying, unseen force responsible for everything created. It was believed that every thought, idea, and invention was communicated by, and caught from, this invisible realm in which the *Logos* existed.[5]

John then, in his Gospel account, proclaims Jesus as the visible, physical manifestation of God when he points out,

The Word [Logos] *became flesh and made His dwelling among us. We have seen His glory, the glory of the One and Only, who came from the Father, full of grace and truth* (John 1:14 NIV).

Throughout the Book of Acts, *logos* refers to the message itself, which is Jesus. Certainly, the apostles used Scripture to validate what they were preaching, but they were not preaching the Bible. Proclaiming the *"Word of God"* meant proclaiming the message of Jesus, the *Logos* of God. In Hebrews 4:12, it is Jesus, the *"Word (Logos) of God,"* not the Scriptures (*graphe*), who is living and active, and sharper than any double-edged sword.

Rhema, then, as it relates to living on every word (*rhema*) that comes from the mouth of God, has to do with having a conversation with the *Logos*, the creator of communication. Moreover, living to hear His voice, and then hanging on every word He speaks to us brings us into our destiny and blessing in life.

Right now, I release an impartation for you to have a conversation with God, in which you clearly catch His voice. I pray that you would encounter Him in the communion of His presence, so that your communication with Him would bring direction, wisdom, and hope to every area of your life.

HEARING AID #3
HEARING TO HEAR

Some people are just *hard of hearing.*

A normal human can hear between 20 and 20,000 hertz, meaning that there are certain ultrasonic and subsonic sounds that we cannot hear. Dogs can hear up to 60,000 hertz, which is why they respond to certain sound frequencies that we cannot discern. Mice hear up to 90,000 hertz, which accounts for their ears being so large in proportion to their bodies. Elephants, on the other hand, can hear subsonic frequencies miles away that we cannot hear even an inch away.[6]

We were designed to hear God's voice. In John 10, Jesus pointed out that His sheep knew His voice and listened to His voice (see John 10:3-4). Interestingly, sheep are near-sighted, but they have an overdeveloped sense of hearing, enabling them to discern their shepherd's voice apart from all others. In the same way, Christians are able to tune in to the frequency of God's voice.

While we are designed to hear God's voice, there still seems to be a choice involved. In Psalm 78:1 the Lord pleads, *"O My people, hear My teaching; listen to the words of My mouth"* (NIV). Jesus implored, *"He who has ears, let him hear…"* (Matt. 11:15 NIV).

Speaking to the thirty-plus year old church of Laodicea, Jesus made an announcement:

> *Here I am! I stand at the door and knock. If anyone hears My voice and opens the door, I will come in and eat with him, and he with Me* (Revelation 3:20 NIV).

Some people have difficulty hearing God's voice because they are on the wrong frequency; they have tuned out God's voice. In reality, God is always standing at the door of our lives, speaking, even when we do not hear Him.

As a teenager, I developed a penchant for tuning out my parents' voice when they were doling out household chores for the day. Later, when confronted about not doing them, I was genuinely honest in saying that I did not hear their requests. I had the capacity to hear their voice, but I had developed selective hearing—their words just did not register.

Not only do we have a choice in whether or not we tune in to God's voice, but it is also a daily decision to develop our hearing competency. Much like a person who is blind and overcompensates by developing his or her sense of hearing, I have learned to develop an acuity for hearing God's voice: I cannot see Him, but I can clearly hear His voice.

Similarly, some people have difficulty discerning the *meaning* of what they are hearing; they cannot seem to catch what is being said. Jesus observed this phenomenon among the people of His time when He pointed out, *"Though hearing, they do not hear"* (Matt. 13:13 NIV).

There is a huge difference between hearing the frequency of sound and understanding what is being said. While we have been created to hear God's voice, not everyone hears what God is saying. We must seek to understand the meaning of the message we are hearing; we must learn to listen in order to *hear* what God is saying.

In 1966, Paul Simon recorded the hit song, "Sounds of Silence," in which he laments the reality that people everywhere are "hearing without listening." Interestingly, people can hear words without getting the message of the words spoken.

The prophet Jeremiah had this complaint when he asked, *"Which of them has stood in the counsel of the lord to see or to hear His word? Who has listened and heard His word?"* (Jer. 23:18 NIV). In other words, who got the meaning of what was said? Who was listening to hear the underlying message?

In 2008, a group launched the National Day of Listening, which is celebrated the day after Thanksgiving. Obviously, there are people concerned that not enough of us are listening these days. Thus, we need a reminder.

We also need help. Jesus promised that the Holy Spirit would guide us into all truth by disclosing what He will say (see John 16:13-15). In other words, the Holy Spirit will help us hear the message encrypted in the words. In addition, we have the Scriptures (see 2 Tim. 3:16), as well as gifted people (see Eph. 4:11-15), to help us understand the truth of what God is saying.

As mentioned earlier, some people completely miss the message of the words they hear. We must be able to hear the truth, and nothing but the truth, if we are going to truly catch God's voice.

God only tells the truth; He cannot lie.

Unfortunately, some people have believed a lie about what God has said and what He is currently saying. We must be able to discern between the truth and lies about the message we hear if we truly want to catch God's voice.

A sure way of identifying a lie is to compare it with the truth of God's nature and character revealed in His many names. For example, if a person with cancer hears, "I [God] have given you this cancer to teach you a lesson [or to keep you humble]," it is a lie. God does not give people cancer. He is not the author of sickness. He is Yahweh Rapha, *"The LORD who heals you"* (Exod. 15:26 NIV). Furthermore, Jesus was clear: Satan is the one who comes to steal, kill, and destroy, while Jesus always brings life (see John 10:10).

A dying woman with fourth stage breast cancer came to me during a healing conference that I was doing in Detroit, Michigan.

She explained that she could not be healed because God had specifically told her that He had given the cancer to teach her humility so that she would rely on Him alone. After several minutes, I interrupted to tell her that she had believed a lie.

Shocked, she assured me that God had clearly spoken to her. As I began to explain the truth of who God is—that He is good, and does good things, and how He wanted to heal her, not kill her, she began to weep as she was set free by the truth of God's word.

When I prayed for her, I could sense God's healing presence being supernaturally absorbed into her body. She felt God's presence as well, and said that her entire body felt strengthened and pain free. A few weeks later, she informed me that her doctor confirmed that there was no more cancer!

I believe this woman was able to receive healing because she was able to hear the true message that Jesus was speaking to her. In truth, when we truly hear Him, the words He speaks will not return empty, but will accomplish what He desires, and achieve the purpose for which He sent them (see Isa. 55:11).

Similarly, when I heard Theresa's voice on the phone, those many years ago, I knew I had truly heard from the Lord. Not only was I flooded with confidence in the direction for my relationship with Theresa, but I was also empowered to fulfill that destiny, through the unique way in which God spoke to me.

In conclusion, the more we hunger to hear God's voice in the context of a continual conversation, the more we will be able to recognize His voice. Similarly, the more we develop spiritual active listening skills, the more we will be able to discern the underlying messages He wants to communicate with us. It is only then that we will truly catch His voice. It is only then that we will fulfill our true God-given destiny.

Happy hearing!

ENDNOTES

1. "100 Fascinating Facts You Never Knew About the Human Brain," *Nursing Assistant Central* Dec. 31, 2009, http://www.nursingassistantcentral.com; accessed April 5, 2010.

2. "Hunger." *Merriam-Webster Online Dictionary.* 2010. *Merriam-Webster Online.* http://www.merriam -webster.com/dictionary/hunger; accessed April 7, 2010).

3. W.E. Vine, *Vine's Expository Dictionary of New Testament Words* (McLean, VA: MacDonald Publishing Company, 1940), 1253. [Note: this one is without copyright.]

4. Gerhard Kittle, *Theological Dictionary of the New Testament* (Grand Rapids, MI: Erdmans, 1964), 69-136.

5. *Ibid.*

6. Wikipedia contributors, "Hearing range," *Wikipedia, The Free Encyclopedia,* http://en.wikipedia.org/w /index.php?title=Hearing_range&oldid=353400124; accessed April 5, 2010.

MORE ABOUT
AUTHOR KEVIN DEDMON

KEVIN DEDMON has been in pastoral ministry for over 25 years and has a B.A. in Biblical Studies and a M.A. degree in Church Leadership from Vanguard University. Kevin oversees the Firestarter Class, which equips and empowers newcomers and new believers to live as revivalists—healing the sick, prophesying, and supernatural evangelism. He is also the director of Bethel Church's Firestorm ministry, which sends teams to local churches for the purpose of demonstrating the revival culture of Bethel Church, as well as imparting, empowering, and activating the church to live naturally in the supernatural, so that the atmosphere in both the church and the community is transformed. Kevin also speaks at conferences and churches worldwide, focusing on healing and supernatural evangelism. He also teaches revival theology in the School of Supernatural Ministry, and trains new believers and new members in a revival supernatural lifestyle in his Firestarter's class at Bethel Church in Redding, California. Kevin is the author of *The Ultimate Treasure Hunt*, and *Unlocking Heaven: Keys to Living Naturally Supernatural*.

7

LIVING FROM HIS PRESENCE

By Rob Coscia

Few people have the imagination for reality.

—GOETHE

Jesus said, "You feed them." And the disciples answered, "You're kidding, right?" —Mark 6:37 (author's paraphrase).

God talks to me in the shower. Not *only* in the shower; He does speak to my heart in other places, but some of my strongest personal encounters with His presence in the supernatural have been when I am at my most vulnerable in the natural. So there I was, rinsing shampoo out of my hair, when I was struck with a powerful image; it was a clear picture of myself at age 4 or 5, standing next to a fish tank... with a hammer.

It was a real memory, but something that I hadn't thought consciously about since I was a kid. We had a 10-gallon fish tank at the top of the stairs, full of goldfish. The hammer in my hand was one of those wooden workbench toys that today are made of plastic, for good reason. I was tapping on the tank, trying to get the attention of the fish, and enjoying the sound the hammer made on the glass. I liked the fish. I liked the quiet, comforting sound of the filter. I would sit and watch them swim and eat, and it gave me a secure feeling as a child.

It didn't break all at once. It cracked with a snap-crunch into a spider-web pattern, leaking water onto the carpet. I helplessly tried to stop it with my hands, like the Little Dutch Boy who stuck his finger in the dyke to stop the flood. No such luck. The tank broke with a large pop, and our staircase was instantly turned into a cascading waterfall, little orange fish bouncing down the steps like misshapen rubber balls toward the front door. My mother came running at the sound, and seeing the look of terror and grief on my face, did not get upset, especially after seeing that I wasn't hurt. We saved as many fish as we could, grabbing the flopping, gasping little creatures and putting them into a bowl of water. She spent the rest of the morning cleaning the mess I had made. I spent the rest of the morning sobbing.

The shower was getting cold, but I didn't care. I was lost somewhere between the vividness of the memory and wondering why God would show me this. Suddenly, there was a question in my head: *"Why do you say you aren't good with tools?"* I have always believed this about myself. I grew up in a foodie family: restaurants, catering, and the like. So I am good with a knife, whisk, or spatula, but I have felt inadequate next to a "real man" who can build things with power saws, drills, and…hammers. I realized that the child who broke the tank with a hammer chose to agree with a lie that presented itself at that moment—that he was clumsy, stupid, and never going to be able to use tools correctly. Right behind that revelation came another, and it hit me hard.

I was mortified by the suffering of the fish. Now, fish are dumb; I knew they weren't taking this personally and plotting revenge against me. Fish are also, in general, tasty. It wasn't so traumatic an event in my childhood that I became a vegetarian. But the sight of the fish struggling for oxygen caused me to agree with another lie, or series of lies. I really did want to just say hello, to connect, to get a response. But staring me in the face was this evolved belief that I was inadequate in relating to the living world; I lived in constant fear that I would let people down, hurt them, fail them no matter how hard I tried, because I was not good enough.

"So, do you want to know what I think about it?" The Lord's voice came to my heart in a wave of peace, washing the anxiety away.

Tears mixed with the cool flow from the shower. "Yes. Please."

I saw my younger self again, but this time Jesus was kneeling beside me. When He spoke, it was to the past and the present me at the same time.

"I know what you were trying to do—you were just saying hello! There was no evil intent in your heart. You are not flawed in relating to My world. I created you to be brilliant in relating to others; the only limitations on you are those that you have placed on yourself. You don't even have a limitation on using tools." He smiled. *"Do you want to know how I see you?"* I nodded, my heart beating faster. "You really are a fish-tank breaker! You will free My people

from their limiting beliefs, from lies, from ungodly thinking, and release them into My river!"

I was overwhelmed; my self-doubts came rushing up their well-established pathways to the surface with signs blazing: *This is only your imagination. Not real. You really do suck at using a hammer.* But the Lord was not giving a place for my inner objections to establish control, and continued, saying, *"My son, so that you know this is real, go look in the mirror."*

I got out of the shower and picked up my towel. Though the water had cooled off, the mirror was still fogged from steam, and I wiped the wet from the glass until I could see my face. It was covered in gold sparkles. I have been to Bible college, a couple of them, in fact, and I'm pretty sure we didn't cover this. "Bathroom Theology" and "Sparkles 101" were just not part of the curriculum. Personally, I file it under *Signs, Wonders, and Crazy-Stuff-God-Does-to-Mess-Me-Up.*

The sparkles lasted most of the day. At dinner, my wife and I told our teenagers about it. They got sparkles. We told our church. Many of them got sparkles. Gold, silver, diamond, multi-colored. My kids went to Brazil on a missions trip. Brazil got sparkled.

I know the Great Commission is not "Go Forth and Bedazzle the Earth," but this event had a tremendous impact on the way that I see God and how I perceive He wants to move through me. What I continue to take away from this isn't a desire for glitter, but an unquenchable desire to know Him. To know that His heart toward me was for a relationship beyond anything I had experienced before was overwhelming and life-changing. I love studying His Word. I love preaching it. I have experience with many areas of ministry. I like history and theoretical physics, and I can intelligently discuss politics and culture. But everything I know, everything I encounter, passes through the filter of living in and from His presence.

We must not apologize for seeking encounters with Him, for seeking to hear Him for ourselves. We must not back down from pursuing Him *personally*, not just academically. I think most people would nod assent with that, but in practice we discourage each other, and ourselves, all the time. We teach people to be afraid of being deceived in ways that keep them so afraid of misrepresenting or failing Him that they do nothing but sit still and wait for God to return, like the servant who buried the one talent. Past failures and fears are like prison walls that keep potentially brilliant people locked in a mindset that sees God as unknowable and themselves as unremarkable or even unlovable.

That He would deal with a root belief system in my life with such love and grace and power tells me that He is absolutely knowable, and that every believer is a uniquely loved son or daughter with an inheritance that we have barely begun to realize. I don't think it's an overstatement to say much of the Church is in a long-distance relationship with God. It's little more than an arranged marriage, and we haven't even met the groom face-to-face yet. Our inheritance *is* the relationship with Him. It is, or should be, as emotionally and spiritually intimate as the wedding night of life-long loves. There we find the answers we have been striving for without Him. There is where our destiny is revealed.

I love King David. He was the ultimate warrior/poet, the man after God's own heart. What impacts me the most personally is a verse in Second Samuel 7. David has become king after 15 or so years of insane training for the job. The Ark, the seat of God's presence, has come into the city at last, and David wants to build a temple around it. The Lord tells David through Nathan the prophet that the temple will be built through his son instead, and then proceeds to tell David what God thinks of him. Nathan paints a picture for David of a dynasty established in peace, of a line that will not end, and of God's everlasting love for him.

David is overwhelmed. In verse 18, the Ark is sitting in a tent. Disregarding all decorum and precepts, David goes in and just plops himself down in front of the Lord, worshiping and thanking God. In verse 19, David says "Is this what You're going to do with all men?" In other words, "We really get to experience You like this? Is this what You've planned all along? Is this what is to come? You will speak to our identity, and as we agree with You, You accomplish the destiny that fullness of identity brings?"

David sat down before God, not out of irreverence, but with the boldness that intimacy creates. This is the boldness that the writer of Hebrews is talking about when approaching the throne of grace. It's the same boldness the apostles prayed for when preaching—but it's not just about speaking daringly to people, it's a state of awareness of His presence, of what you carry, of the substance of the Kingdom, so that you are living from His presence.

I'm not talking about open-heaven encounters as a fad, a wave, a new theology, an ancient mystic secret, a gimmick to sell books, or a "50-dollar-donation-gets-you-the-deluxe-prayer-cloth" infomercial. Nor am I against a systematic study of Scripture, Bible colleges, denominations, or solid theology. But I am positive that anything I learn that does not lead me to an opportunity for an encounter with the Lord is suspect as man's ideas and not His. It is the seizing of those opportunities that we must have a passion for. I love to see people go after Him, and I love to encourage them to try and manifest every revelation of His nature and character He has shown them. The knowledge of Him may point us in the right direction, but it is in the pursuit of Him that we become free.

I was a new Christian in a Bible college in Louisiana, sitting in a first-period Old Testament Survey class. The quiet, humble teacher was describing Moses' snake-on-a-stick health clinic, then stopped midway and asked if anyone was feeling ill. Several students raised their hands, and the rest of the class (and most of the next) turned into one of the first experiences I had with supernatural healing. Sometime later, I took a class in a different Bible university that covered the same portion of Scripture. The professor was brilliant and dynamic, and gave us the alliterative 7 "P"s, or something like that, of obedience in the wilderness. I can't remember one of them at the moment. I will never forget the open heaven the first teacher opened up.

It's an opinion based on 20 years of ministry, and not a statement of survey and research, but I believe that leaders in the Church don't promote more personal encounters with God mainly because of their own insecurity. The source of that insecurity is vast, from stress-filled, perceived expectations to rigid belief systems that have choked the joy of real relationships out of their calling. The results are damaging no matter the root. When we are insecure, not at rest, not at peace, we approach almost everything with either fear or anger or both. In that frame of mind, I cannot allow anyone to be more powerful than me spiritually. They are a threat to my position.

Pastors and leaders want to protect the flock, which is noble. But when we are insecure in our own relationship with God, we often interpret that to mean we protect people from anything that isn't in our experience or control. Instead of exhorting people to be accountable to the dreams that God has put in them, we hold people accountable to our fears. We have learned that our worth as a pastor is tied directly to perceiving ourselves as the most powerful person in the room, spiritually and usually intellectually. If someone says they have heard God in a way that takes away from our feeling of worth, it's a threat. I must cut off threats—rationalizing my thoughts and actions by saying it so they can't damage anyone. We teach fear. We teach others to be so afraid of thinking outside our doctrinal and denominational distinctives that no one is free to grow into anything but what the pastor deems is safe.

Many of us have had experience with someone who has some kind of "special knowledge," a self-proclaimed prophet that is not accountable to anyone and responsible for none of his actions because "God told him." People like that are wolves that require discernment, wisdom, and courage to deal with; many have done real damage in the Body of Christ. But putting constraints on the freedom people have in Christ, in the name of avoiding wolves and deception, has caused great casualties. We have somehow got it into our heads that people pursuing Him for themselves will result in rebellion and anarchy. We are so worried that someone might do something differently than what was done in the past that we limit people from becoming what God may be training them for. At best, it's identity theft. At worst, it's spiritual abortion.

God has no chaos; the fruit of pursuing Him isn't division and destruction. The key is living in an atmosphere secure in the Father's love, because others will then have the freedom to do the same around me. The fruit of the Spirit is natural in that environment. The gifts of the Spirit flow without qualification. Love is organic, because He is Love itself. Everything in

His Kingdom works through relationship; consequently, when people have the freedom to know Him to the fullness of who they were created to be, the result is the Body of Christ, not a dismembered horror show.

It must be our goal that people become brilliant, and that they have permission to go far beyond us in knowing and loving Him. And, we just have to deal with the fact that there is just no way that's going to happen in an un-messy, controlled way. We made mistakes, but instead of just sharing our journey so others can learn from our mistakes, we try to keep others from making any of their own. That's not the Gospel, because that's not freedom. We have super-talented people sitting in front of us every Sunday, but we see them only in terms of how they can serve our vision, instead of asking God what each person was created for and how we can encourage and equip His vision for them. We must be about freedom. We must understand that if we teach people to hear God for themselves, we win!

I choose to live my life in His presence by consciously stewarding the freedom that Jesus has purchased for me. He said that He is the Way, the Truth, the Life. Living aware of His desire for me to know Him at deeper and deeper levels means I get to experience Him in each of those manifestations of His character and nature; I can ask Him to reveal Himself as Truth in my life. I know someone will argue that He will do that anyway. But there is a huge difference between seeing ourselves as He does, from His reality, and seeing ourselves from our own.

His world has nothing missing. Nothing broken. When He shows up as Truth in a situation, it is to bring love and restoration and freedom. The woman caught in adultery in John 8 knew her guilt, she knew the truth of the law that others judged her with. But Jesus showed up as the Truth. Her sins didn't frighten or shock Him; He saw from Heaven's perspective who she really was, what she was capable of becoming. Those about to stone her lived in a mindset of religious control, working from earth toward Heaven. Their fear demanded punishment to maintain their sense of (in)security. In Jesus' challenge for those without sin to cast the first stone, there was also an invitation to see as He sees. But they refused, only seeing a greater truth outwit theirs, like a debate. But for the woman, the Truth literally set her free.

If I had remembered breaking that fish tank without seeing it from His perspective, I would have judged it as a condemnation, a failure right at the beginning of my life. I may have been able to understand the root of my tool-phobia, but without His presence to bring truth to the situation, I would still feel powerless to do much about it. That's how so many of us live, especially in church. We go every week, maybe twice and do what we are told we should do, but there is this draining malaise behind our Sunday smiles that is wondering how this could be all there is, especially when deep down we know there must be more.

Thoreau wrote, "Most men lead lives of quiet desperation, and go to their graves with the song still in them." It's a powerful observation of many who sell their true selves cheaply to conform to what they perceive is expected of them, though it be unsatisfying, stressful, limiting, disempowering, and counter to their true persona, their song. To choose to live as a slave should simply not be acceptable to you, especially when there are millions for whom slavery and abject poverty are not a choice, those who are looking for those who are already free to lead them to freedom.

HEALING IN AISLE SEVEN

I was in one of the big-box home repair stores; my list of things to do that day was long and so I was walking as fast as I could to find...Wham! I felt as though I had just walked into a wall of water. The feeling flowed from my head through my chest, a rush of blood and a tingle of nerves. I stopped and did a quick evaluation of myself. It wasn't pain, it was...I looked around, and there was a woman carefully studying bolt sizes. I walked past her, and the feeling hit me again. OK, Lord, so what do you have for her? A picture of a spine popped in my head.

I am, by nature, an introvert. I have been through evangelism courses that were sheer torture for my personality; they expected you to ambush people like a used car salesman in a rhinestone cowboy hat and alligator boots. I like people and I like talking, but if I have no freedom to speak out of my own heart and experiences with God, I feel completely disempowered. Life in the Kingdom is so different.

"Excuse me, I'm sorry to bother you, but...are you having back pain?"

She looked at me with shock. "How did you know that?"

"God just told me." I've had lots of different responses to that statement, but hers was unexpected, and awesome.

"Oh, He did hear me! I was desperately praying this morning for some answers in my and my husband's life." In my mind, I saw a tractor-trailer.

"Are you long-distance drivers?" Her tearful response told me I was hearing Him. For the next few minutes, I related encouragement and blessing as God gave them to me for her and her husband. We prayed for her back which was severely damaged, and though she wasn't completely healed, she felt enormous physical relief, and could bend over for the first time in quite awhile. Freedom came to aisle seven.

Heidi Baker said: "I want to live as if I am hidden in His very heart, where His thoughts become my thoughts and His ways become my ways. This is how we will reach the world." That isn't a pithy quote for an encouragement poster. It's our blood-bought birthright. We reach the world from the overflow of our relationship with Him. The more we steward His voice in our lives, aligning our thinking to how He thinks, the more impact we have on everyone we meet.

One of the greatest secrets of the throne room is that you are a throne room. You are a living tabernacle, a mobile re-presentation of God. You're an RV, a resurrection vehicle, a revelation vehicle, a revolution vehicle. Pick your favorite 'R' word out of your concordance. You are the royal priesthood, who dwells in the tabernacle ministering to Him, and out of that overflow comes everything you need to be brilliant in this world.

When Jesus ministered to the 5,000 men, plus who knows how many women and children, the disciples raised concerns over the crowds needing food. He told His disciples to feed them.

"Um, excuse me, Jesus? I'm not sure we heard you correctly, Lord. It's so loud with all these people, and all. Did you mean you wanted us to call for pizza? 'Cause that's cool, but I don't think they're gonna make it in 30 minutes…."

"No, I told you to give them something to eat."

Jesus blessed the bread and fish, but it was the disciples who fed everyone. (See Matt. 14:13-21.) In the overflow of His love and grace, of His Kingdom thinking and purposes, of His nature and character, we become His living manifestations of all of those and more. Countless times Jesus taught them by word and action how to live from His presence while interacting with this world.

When the sparkles started appearing, I had, for over a year, diamond-like sparkles ingrained into two pages of my Bible in the book of Acts. They were part of the paper and couldn't be rubbed away, although several people who touched them got sparkles on their hands and their Bibles. I asked Him what He was highlighting for me. In my heart, I heard "5:20": "Go and stand in the temple courts and proclaim to the people all the words of this life" (author's paraphrase, see Acts 5:20). This is what we get to do! We are living temples; everyone we encounter is in our courts!

Think about that for a moment. If this is true, that we are really invited to live this close to Him, then every problem, every opportunity, every relationship really can be approached from God's perspective. Everywhere you look, you are as powerful as you are aware of His presence in any given situation. The most powerful people on the planet are those who will steward the freedom and the gifts they have been given by living consciously aware of His presence. This is a challenging time in history; the world is looking for those with the answers that come from that awareness.

The Lord is not defensive. He is not a coward. So it is an offense to the Captain of Angel Armies that the Church chooses to become Chicken Little when faced with difficult circumstances. When American culture started shifting visibly and dramatically in the 1960s and '70s, the Church's response was to declare the end of the world. This was the last generation, so go home and wait for the Lord to show up and rescue you. But instead of the

Rapture, unbelieving, bitter people took over any area that the church abandoned. Anytime there is a space, something is going to fill it. The mess in my garage proves it. If we are not willing to let the Lord train us to excel brilliantly in every sphere of our world, then the enemy will be delighted to take our place.

Courage without encounter is fleeting. His nature is valiant, and we can live valiantly as well. Not a life of yo-yo reactions to circumstances, but powerfully and consistently as we walk aware of Him in us. The creativity and leadership the planet is searching for is already here. It's in you. Let Him draw it out of you and train you in it. Psalm 18 is David's recounting of God saving him at a particularly difficult time; "You rescued me because You delighted in me" (see Ps. 18:19). The rest of the psalm is David being trained by God Himself to attack those that had nearly destroyed him.

David's encounters with God enabled David to think differently about his situation and prepared him to reign. When the enemy stole the families and possessions of himself and his men, his army nearly collapsed in grief and anguish, even to the point they were considering killing David. In First Samuel 30:6 it says, *"But David strengthened himself in the LORD"* (NKJV). That word *strengthen* means "to seize, to lay hold of"—what? A principle? A rule? A song? David laid hold of the God he knew face-to-face. He knew this loss was not the work of the God whose character and nature had been revealed to him time and time again. He knew the only thing that would make any sense would have to come from God's mouth. "Pursue. Overtake. Recover all." (See First Samuel 30:8.) David's perception of the situation from God's reality shifted the atmosphere for thousands and won back even more than what was taken.

I was an ROTC student at a university in the Northeast. I was a good cadet and loved the program. One day the command staff introduced us to SERE, which stands for Survival, Evasion, Resistance, and Escape. SERE is an incredibly intense exercise designed to help military personnel mentally cope with being captured by the enemy in battle. We were being invited to volunteer to participate in a scaled-down version.

Forty of us college freshmen and sophomores met at a military installation a couple of hours away and were released into the woods to be hunted by the upperclassmen cadets, and, as we later found out, by regular army and special forces personnel as well. Almost everyone was found, and those of us who weren't were called in after it got dark. Then the fun started.

All of our captors wore black uniforms with no identifying insignia. We were ordered to call them "brother" and then thrown into a common cell. It's hard to describe adequately the fear that took over; you'd think that since we knew the upperclassmen, and knew each other well, that we could bear this fairly easily. But it got real.

We were never physically beaten, and the one guy who said he was hit was a spy. But we did thousands and thousands of push-ups, sit-ups, leg-lifts, and the like incessantly. Some of us were privileged to have all four limbs handcuffed behind us, with a broom stick stuck through the cuffs to twist to our captors' satisfaction. Others were chained outside in their underwear in the November night air. We were not allowed to sleep. Then the real fun started.

Each of us was brought in turn for individual interrogation multiple times. We were just kids; we had no vital military information, but that's not what they wanted. Their goal was to teach us to mentally hang on to something to keep us from breaking. Any information we gave them meant they owned us. Some broke right away. Others took time. But everyone eventually gave in to the intense mental and physical abuse, or they were tricked into signing *confessions.*

I was failing. This was my second interrogation, and I was tired. I was on my knees before my interrogator, my outstretched arms holding bricks. Behind me was a powerful man with a big knife and a stun gun. I thought I was strong, but all I wanted to do was hide somewhere and sleep. My back was painfully injured during the ongoing *exercises,* and I had very little left in the physical or emotional tank. Then something happened.

I had a belief in God, having grown up in both Catholic and Presbyterian churches. I had accepted Him watching the *700 Club* when I was 16. My parents were both Christians. But I had never had an encounter. As I knelt there, "Brother" tore me apart verbally, shredding any mental strength I had in reserve. Then he said it. Now, as you might imagine, he had been cursing me up and down with every curse I'd ever heard and a bunch that were new to me, but this one I felt.

"Jesus Christ, what a wimp! We heard you were strong! You're nothing!"

As soon as he used the Lord's name like that, as a curse over my failure and weakness, something started to burn inside me. It angered me. He could say whatever he wanted to about me, but not Jesus. For the first time, I looked at him in the eye and glared. He saw what just happened and instantly exploited it.

"Oh, no way! You're not one of *those,* are you? Are you really a Christian?" He laughed derisively.

Time stopped. I was no longer being tortured; I was no longer in that room. I was face-to-face with God. No words were spoken out loud, but I felt them inside me, more real than my own heartbeat.

"I love you."

That's all I needed. I *did* believe, not just about Him; I believed *Him*. I believed what He said. When I came back to myself, I was filled with strength; I straightened up and held the bricks straight out. I locked eyes with my captor. After a lengthy stare-down I knew I would not lose, *he* cracked. He broke eye contact and spoke to the soldier behind me.

"Get him out of here." Out of 40, I was the only one not to break; they used me as an example of finding something to hold onto that is more powerful than what is trying to kill you. But I knew it was more. It was an encounter that would shape the rest of my life. An encounter the likes of which you are invited to anytime. Open heavens aren't something that we hope happens for a half-hour at the end of a service during a scheduled revival after being spiritually beaten up by the sweaty evangelist. Open heaven is what Jesus has written on your head. In sparkles.

Take some time with God and ask Him to show you Himself. You may see a picture, or He may direct you to a Scripture. He may have you write something; don't limit how He can talk to you.

Ask Him if there is anything He wants to show you about yourself. He is always loving, always restorative, and always brilliant. Often funny, too. He is patient, kind, generous, joyful, and His thoughts toward you are good. You are amazing. You are powerful. You are loved. Ask Him to help you rethink what's possible. Determine to live and love aware of His presence.

How do you know it's Him? Do you feel real peace? Do you feel closer to Him, more in love with Him? Do you feel empowered and connected to your identity and purpose? That's Him. Write down what you see, hear, etc., and pray on it until it becomes manifested, and give it away.

MORE ABOUT
AUTHOR ROB COSCIA

Rob Coscia and his wife Angi have been in ministry for twenty years. They are lead pastors of Diamond Valley Church, located in Northeastern Pennsylvania. Rob is ordained with Global Awakening. He was educated at Wilkes University in Wilkes-Barre, Pennyslvania, with degrees in political science and history, and at North Central University in Minneapolis, Minnesota with emphasis on pastoral ministry. Rob and Angi have two amazing children, Kim and Rob.

8

THE KEY TO PRODUCING A CROP

By Bruce Van Natta

When I was originally asked to be part of this writing project, I was told that it was to be about hearing God's voice and the official title had not been chosen yet. I had already written a whole book on hearing God's voice, but I didn't want to base this chapter on just my "old" material. I began to pray for the Lord to give me some "fresh" revelation knowledge that I could share with you, the readers, but wasn't getting anything. One day, I shut myself up in my bedroom and climbed on top of our bed with a notebook and pen and told the Lord I wasn't going to move until He spoke something. I prayed for quite awhile with not much happening and have to admit I started to get sleepy. At the point I was about to fall asleep the Lord gave me a very simple vision.

It was a vision of a large "ear" of corn. The husk was still on it but had been pulled back in one spot to reveal the golden kernels of ripe corn underneath. It vanished, and I asked the Lord what it meant. Then the Holy Spirit spoke and said, "He who has *ears* let him hear" (see Matt. 13:9). I chuckled at God's sense of humor and obvious use of a pun, but had to admit to Him that I didn't understand what He was saying! The Holy Spirit spoke again and told me that when we hear *and* understand His "word" we will produce a crop and then told me to go to the parable of the four soils and He would show me something I hadn't seen before. Much of the following chapter is based on what He began to show me about a parable that I always thought was only to do with salvation.

In Matthew chapter 13, Mark chapter 4, and Luke chapter 8, Jesus tells the parable of the four soils and then gives His disciples the meaning of it. If we study all four accounts, we can get a clearer picture of what Jesus is saying.

He talks about a farmer who went out to sow his seed. As he did, some fell on the path and was eaten by the birds. Some seed fell on rocky ground where it sprang up quickly, but ended up withering because it had no root. Some seed fell among thorns, which grew and choked the plants, and some seed fell on good soil where it produced a crop a hundred, sixty, or thirty times what was sown.

Jesus tells us in Luke 8:11 that the seed is the "Word" of God. The Greek word for *Word* here is *Logos*. According to the Strong's concordance, this is a spoken or written communication with a focus on the content (often about who God is or what He is like). He goes on to explain that the four types of soil represent the four ways that people can respond to the "word," or again some type of communication from God including who He is and what He is like.

We learn that the first group is those who hear about God or from God but don't understand. They, therefore, don't believe and the "word" is snatched from them.

The second group is those who hear a message about the kingdom and receive it with joy, until a time of testing comes and then they fall away from the "word."

The third group of people is compiled of those who hear the "word," but are choked by life's worries, riches, and pleasures, and they do *not mature* and are *unfruitful*.

Jesus says this about the last group of people in Matthew 13:23, "*...the seed that fell on good soil is the man **who hears the word and understands it**. **He produces a crop**, yielding a hundred, sixty or thirty times what was sown*" (NIV). The other Gospel accounts add that this group of people not only heard the "word" and understood it, but they **accepted** it, **retained** it, and **persevered** to produce a crop.

This parable or message was so important that Jesus said that if a person didn't know or understand this parable that they wouldn't be able to know or understand *any* parable! (See Mark 4:13.)

Why was this message so important? I believe that Jesus placed such emphasis on this parable for two big reasons. It not only explains how all people can and will react to a salvation message about God, but it also defines the **principle truths** as to how a person responds to the specific messages, or individual "words" from God and what outcome that has on their life and the Kingdom! Either they will be fruitful in that particular area, or they will not.

Jesus clearly says that we need to not only **hear His voice, but to understand it** in order to produce a crop and be fruitful.

Remember that when we looked at all three Gospel accounts of the parable we found that Jesus clarified this truth by saying that we would **accept** the "word," **retain** it, and **persevere** until we produced a crop. It is clear from Scripture that this principle truth extends to every area of our lives and therefore the Kingdom as a whole.

So if a person who fit into the first category, or way of responding, heard a salvation message, they wouldn't understand or believe it and, therefore, would not get saved. If a person from the second category heard a salvation message they would accept Jesus into their heart until something bad happened, at which point they would entirely give up on God and reject Him. When a person from the third category hears a salvation message they accept it, but Jesus says that they never mature and remain unfruitful because of various reasons. When the people from the last category hear a salvation message, they hear and understand it—accepting it, retaining it, and persevering or abiding in Him until they produce a crop. This crop would start as their own personal salvation, but could then include countless other things such as helping to bring others to faith, showing love, working of miracles, etc.

OUR DAILY CHOICES

Let's see what the principle truths from this parable look like in our day-to-day existence as a Christian. The four groups or categories that Jesus pointed out are simply four different ways we can respond to His "words." Just because we respond one way to something He is telling us doesn't mean that we will respond that same way to another thing He tries to tell us. So even though we might be hearing, understanding, and bearing fruit in one area of our life, we can be resisting God, (either knowingly or unknowingly) in another situation and therefore be unfruitful in that region. So we could be obedient about worshiping Him regularly, but ignore Him when He tries to get us out of our comfort zone in another area, like witnessing for example. If we are honest with ourselves we can also usually think of some areas that we have resisted what the Lord was telling us because we weren't willing to change or respond. We are not always responding to Him in the same method or from the same category.

In fact, just because we have responded in a certain way to a certain "word" doesn't mean that we won't change our response at a later time. As a person goes through different seasons or phases in life, we can see how, at some point, they didn't hear or understand what the Lord was telling them in a certain area until later. For example, many believers didn't know or understand the blessings that come with tithing and giving when they were new believers, but realized its value and importance as they matured in the Lord.

The message or "word" about tithing and giving is a great one to use for an illustration as to how these principle truths from the parable apply to our daily decisions. If a believer chooses the first response type to this topic they would not understand or believe the message about tithing and that truth would be "snatched" from them. They would lose any blessings they could have gotten from following it, and would not be a blessing in that area to others either.

When a believer chooses the second response type, they would hear about tithing and begin to do it for a short time, but as soon as finances looked tight or they didn't receive some immediate benefits, they would quickly stop. There would be no fruit or crop with this choice as well.

A believer who chooses the third response type would hear about tithing and begin to do it for a season, but after they realized how much their tithe totaled over time, they would start to think about all the other things they could do with that money (a new vehicle, an exotic vacation, pay off the mortgage, more for the retirement plan, a new deck, unpaid bills, etc.) and they would talk themselves out of continuing to tithe and give regularly.

The believer who chooses the last way of responding to God's "Word" about tithing and giving would not only understand the concept, but would begin to follow this plan. They would also decide that no matter what, they were not going to stop giving back to the Lord. As the days, months, and years passed, they would remain faithful to this commitment and would begin to see a harvest or crop of blessings come back to them in many ways, just as the Lord has promised. (See 2 Corinthians 9:6-15.)

This is why it is so important to be able to **hear** what the Lord is saying to us and also be able to **understand** how we are to apply that knowledge, so that we can be blessed and be a blessing to others! Every Christian in the right frame of mind should want to be in the center of the Lord's will for their life, hearing and understanding Him so that they can lead a fruitful life.

HEARING GOD

We can't understand or even know what the Lord is saying to us unless we can hear Him. So hearing God is the first step or foundation for everything that is Kingdom minded. Sadly, there are many Christians around the world who would honestly say that they have never heard the Lord speak to them. Yet, Jesus tells us in John 8:47, *"He who belongs to God hears what God says"* (NIV). How can we explain this discrepancy?

From what I have encountered, I believe that, although there are many answers to that question, one stands out above the rest: people's expectations and assumptions as to how God speaks. Some think that God has told people all He is ever going to and that He has no perceivable interaction with his followers on a personal level any more. Then there are those who believe that if God were to speak to you it would be absolutely unmistakable, thunder and lightning would be going off, the earth would be shaking, and a loud voice would come from the sky that would penetrate you to your very core. Although God can and sometimes does speak to people this way, it is the exception, not the "norm." Often, when God speaks to us, we could easily miss it if we weren't paying attention and listening for Him.

If we were to look at every single example in the Bible of when the Lord communicated with someone, we would see that sometimes He did it directly while at other times it was indirectly. We would also find that all of these instances could be put in one of seven different categories or methods that God uses to speak to people. He meant it when He said *"I the LORD do not change"* (Mal. 3:6 NIV). He will speak to us today in the same ways He spoke to those in the Bible..

We don't want to ever try to put God in a box or limit Him by narrowly defining these broad categories, but we do want to see what He has done in the past so that we can know what to expect in the future. The following seven categories describe the ways that we can anticipate the Lord to speak to us today.

By knowing how we can expect Him to speak to us, we can better understand how to hear Him.

1. **God talks through the process of prayer.** While this may sound very elementary, it is actually much deeper. When we pray, God hears and answers us. Although it may not always be the answer we want or expect, He will answer and speak through His answers. We can also fully expect to hear Him in the process of praying or talking with Him, which is meant to be a two-way conversation, an exchange.

2. **God talks through the Bible**. Our Lord has given us the Bible so that we may know certain things about Him and our journey in this life. The Bible's verses are His very "words" to us, and we can fully believe that He is speaking to us through all that is written in it. As we read the Bible or even other items that contain the principles found in Scripture, we can expect to hear God speaking directly to us about our individual and specific needs, wants, or issues.

3. **God talks through the spoken Word**. God can speak to you through the preacher at church, on television, or on the radio. He can give you a message through your parent, spouse, or children. God can and will even use surprising outlets to deliver His "word" to us. The source is not important; we must remember the power is in the message not the messenger. We need to be ready to hear God speak to us whether it is through a stranger, friend, or even an enemy.

4. **God talks through the Holy Spirit**. The number of ways that the Lord can speak to us through the Holy Spirit is uncountable. It could be anything from an audible voice to a thought, from an inner whisper to a feeling, from a perception to a physical sensation. It can be an awareness or discernment of things in the natural

or spiritual realm. No matter what way the Holy Spirit speaks to us, a receptive heart can expect to hear Him day in and day out!

5. **God talks through design and circumstance.** The Bible tells us that God speaks to us through all of creation or nature, from the big things to the little things. His design carries over into even our circumstances, or what some might call fate or destiny. God is able to weave His divine plan throughout the generations despite the devil, bad choices, or our sin. There is no such thing as coincidence, and we need to hear what God is saying even through the mundane.

6. **God talks through dreams and visions.** While not every dream or vision we have is from God, the Lord continues to communicate with us whether we are awake or asleep. Sometimes dreams are quite literal, and we will know exactly what they mean. At other times, they are more symbolic like the parables are, and we will need the Holy Spirit to interpret them. We should anticipate hearing from God through our dreams and the images that we see in our mind.

7. **God talks through angels.** The Lord is still sending His angels to this earth. Many believers will testify to feeling their presence, while others whose spiritual eyes have been opened will actually see them. We know from Scripture that we would never worship these beings or believe anything given by one that is contrary to what we find in the Bible. They are God's servants and, even if they are silent, we can still hear God speaking to us through their presence.

When we know how we can expect our Lord to speak to us, it puts us in a position of better understanding how to hear Him. It's not even a question as to if He is speaking to us or not. The real question is, *Are we listening to Him?* Are we honestly seeking the Lord and His will for us, and are we trying to hear Him? In other words, are our hearts receptive?

After telling the parable of the four soils, Jesus quotes the Old Testament prophet Isaiah and states in Matthew 13:15 that people whose hearts have become calloused can hardly hear with their ears. He is obviously talking about a person's spiritual ears at this point. Each of us need to examine our heart and see if there are any areas in it that have become calloused and prevented us from hearing everything that the Lord is saying to us. It is rather easy to become deceived in a certain area and the danger is that we wouldn't realize it!

We can become so comfortable with a sin in our life that we don't even think it's wrong, or we can begin to believe that God just winks at that little old sin. I have met people who have continued to pray over an issue that is clearly forbidden in the Bible and then wonder why the Lord isn't granting their improper request, or blessing their sin. The Lord has given us the Scriptures and will not do, say, or bless something that is contrary to them no matter how much we pray for it.

I have seen others who have petitioned the Lord over something that is clearly explained in the Bible and then wondered why the Lord hasn't answered their question. If we claim to be a Christian, He wants and expects us to spend time in the Bible and will sometimes be quiet to force us to search the matter out in His Word.

There are also times where the Lord has spoken something to us and knows full well we have heard Him, but have not acted on what He has said. During those times, He can become seemingly silent for a time, waiting for us to respond to what He has already communicated before moving on to the next thing.

All of us need to be intentional about making ourselves open and available to what the Lord is saying. Remember Jesus told us that we need to accept His "word," retain it, and persevere. These words describe someone who is *actively* engaged in the process. We need to be hungry for the truth and eager to hear Him and respond when He speaks to us, no matter what method He chooses to deliver His *Word*.

UNDERSTANDING GOD

Jesus explained in our parable that we needed to not only hear but also to understand in order to produce a crop. When the Lord first gave me the vision of the ear of corn, I was hearing Him in a way, but still not understanding Him yet. It wasn't until I pressed in further that I was given more information, at which point I was able to understand what the meaning was. The choice was mine and I could have easily dismissed what I saw because I didn't understand it initially.

Jesus said that the people from the first group are those who hear from God but don't understand and, therefore, don't believe. So it is clear we have a choice whether to believe the messages that God gives. Some people will reject what the Lord says because they don't understand it. The Bible tells us not believing a message that the Lord has spoken to us can make it of no value or profit to us (see Heb. 4:2).

Unfortunately, I can think of several times in my own life where this exact thing has happened to me. Sometimes the consequences were not long lasting, while they were permanent at other times.

Several years ago, the Holy Spirit started urging me to go visit two immediate family members at their new house. Although I knew it was the Lord leading me to do this, I didn't know why. I was really struggling with some personal problems that week, so I honestly didn't want to be around anyone at the time.

The next day, the Lord again kept urging me to go over there or to at least call. Because I didn't understand why it was so important, I disregarded it and justified my actions by telling the Lord I would go when I was feeling better. That night, one of the two committed suicide. I had no idea that there were any depression issues with the person and there was nothing in the natural that would have made me even begin to think that something like that was going to happen. I didn't understand the urgency and, therefore, didn't believe that I really needed to go right then.

This is a classic example of what happens when we choose the first response type to a message from God. We hear the "word" but don't understand it and then decide not to believe it. At that point, God's message does not bless us or those it was originally intended to. I am reminded of the reality of that truth every time I see my family member who lost their spouse and how it has affected their life to this day. Thank the Lord for forgiveness when we blow it!

Many Christians would say that they will do their best to be obedient when they are certain that they have heard from the Lord about something. The problem comes when we are not completely certain if we have heard from the Lord or have heard Him correctly. It could be that the impression is brief, or that it doesn't seem to make any sense, or that the Lord is speaking in a way that we are not familiar with.

As I travel around the world ministering, much of what I do is "hands-on ministry" (and "hands-on learning" for that matter). After speaking at a place, I will always invite people forward for prayer if given the chance, and the Lord will often speak to me about the people I am ministering to. I have learned that sometimes the Lord will tell me something that makes no sense in the natural until I begin to act on it. This might mean that I need to begin saying a certain thing or doing a certain thing even if it goes against my natural instincts. There have been times where it has felt like a test to see if I will step out on the water, but I know that the Lord uses these opportunities to prove to me that **I can trust Him even when I don't initially understand Him.** This concept is true for all believers and applies to our entire walk with the Lord!

I will never forget the first time that He gave me a *word* for someone through the use of pain. I had only been in ministry a short time and had traveled to another state to speak. During the early part of the service, my right ankle began to hurt horribly. I prayed for the Lord to take the pain away, but there was no change. The worship ended and it was now time for me to go stand up front to speak. As I began walking up the steps of the altar, I was complaining to the Lord as to why He wouldn't take the pain away, and that still, small whisper told me I didn't understand. It then dawned on me that this might be about someone else. I asked the Lord to take the pain away if it was an injury or attack from the enemy, but to allow it to remain if it was a "word" for somebody who had ankle pain.

As I stood behind the podium, it began to hurt even worse. I had never been in this church before and was told that most of the people in this denomination were a little skeptical about this whole "healing" thing. I had also never prayed for people before speaking; prayer had always come after the message in the past. But I didn't want to have to try and speak with this pain. I asked the audience whose right ankle was hurting so badly that they could barely put any weight on it. A woman right near the front stood up and said it was her. I prayed from where I was, and the Lord instantly healed her ankle and then took the pain away from me also.

Initially, I didn't understand the pain was from the Lord, but after pressing in He made it clear it was. Apparently He didn't want the woman to have to sit through the message with the pain, and, maybe even more importantly, He wanted to set the tone for a very powerful night of ministry. The Lord is speaking to us; and if we want to produce a crop, we need to believe or accept His messages, even when we don't initially understand them.

TIME OF TESTING

Jesus tells us in our parable that the second response to a message from God is to fall away during a time of testing. It is clear from Scripture that there will be times we are tested, and often the Lord will test us concerning something that He has spoken to us just like He did with Abraham with Isaac. These tests can really vary as to what they look like, and many times we won't even recognize them as a test at first.

Maybe a person feels like the Lord has given them a certain verse or promise about an issue, but the problem gets worse instead of better. Some good examples would be Joseph or David. They both were promised positions of leadership, but both got demoted before they were eventually promoted. It was their choice, just as it is our choice if we are going to let go of what the Lord said, or hang on to it and persevere.

Sometimes the Lord will only give us a sliver of information and then expect us to respond in faith. In other words believe that we can accept what He is saying and then act on it. This is just as true for everyday life as it is for ministry. Like the vision of the ear of corn, it could be a simple picture in our mind or it could be just one word that drops in as a thought. The test at these times is, *Will we accept and persevere with what the Lord is saying when it is such a small piece of information?*

Another test this can bring up is, *Will we begin to "fill in the blanks" with our own limited knowledge instead of relying completely on the Lord?* In other words, God speaks something to us, but there aren't many details; so, we begin to try to make sense of it in the natural and add our ideas to God's "word." This is when we can "muddy the water" by making false assumptions.

Once while ministering in Toronto, Canada, I had this very thing happen. Before the service, we were praying and the Lord began to give words of knowledge about people that would be attending. He told us some names, He told us some prayer requests that people had, and then He showed me a very clear picture of the right side of a man's shiny bald head. I saw it as if I were looking down from above and the Lord said that this man's prayer would be answered. We wrote the "words" down as we drove to the church, and I described in detail to my friend the shiny bald head and the odd angle I saw it from.

After speaking that night I started calling out the words of knowledge from the list *before* opening it up for general prayer. Each item on the list was resolved, and the prayers were gloriously answered one by one until we got to the bald-headed vision. I was trying to decide how to call this one out when a man in an electric scooter came up the center aisle and didn't stop until he hit the altar. My blood ran cold as I looked down and saw the right side of his shiny bald head *and* an equally shiny **artificial leg**!

I had not called this word of knowledge out yet, so at that point, I asked the crowd if there were any other bald men in the place with a shiny head. No one else came forward, so I went out in the crowd myself looking for someone else that fit the description. When I couldn't find anybody I came back to the front and handed my partner the microphone. I told him to tell the people what the Lord had told me before the service. He shook his head no. I urged him on so I could hear with my own ears what God had said again. I knew in my spirit God could do a creative miracle and give this man a new leg, but my mind and body were struggling with the idea.

After my friend spoke out what the Lord had shown me and said that the bald man would get his prayer answered, I handed the bald man the microphone and told him to tell everyone what his prayer request was. I looked away knowing that he was about to ask the Lord for a new leg. To my shock, he said he needed deliverance from a certain issue. At this point my faith skyrocketed. When I placed my hands on him and said a quick prayer, the power of God came on him like high voltage electricity; and everyone who saw it agreed that it looked like he had been violently electrocuted. When he woke up a while later, he told us he felt entirely better.

This had clearly been a test for me, and I almost failed it because of my wrong assumptions and fears. This world, the devil, and even our own thoughts will try to get us to doubt what the Lord tells us, but when we hang on to His "word" we can and will pass the tests.

THE THORNS

Jesus said that the third type of response to a message from God was when a person hears the "word" but life's worries, riches, and pleasures choke it, making it unfruitful and the person immature. This is when we know what the Lord has told us, but there is something else that tries to convince us to turn away or turn back from God's "word."

We might immediately think of all of the obvious sinful traps of the world that are there to draw us away from the Lord like drugs, alcohol, sexual temptations, greed, and so on, but the traps can also be more deceptive.

The devil can use "good" things to prevent us from fulfilling the "great" things that God has for us. Our good intentions are useless unless we are guided by the Lord every step of the way. Even after we have gotten a good start of hearing and understanding something from the Lord, we have the ability to throw it away if we don't persevere to the end. During the process, there is a danger we can get off track from the Lord's will if we are not diligent, continuing to abide in Him. Hebrews 12:1-2 says *"…let us throw off everything that hinders and the sin that so easily entangles, and let us run with perseverance the race marked out for us. Let us fix our eyes on Jesus, the author and perfecter of our faith"* (NIV).

I once heard a man speaking who had been setting up a large crusade in India in 2004. He had spent much money making preparations for the event and had already taken one trip over there to do some ministry and get things ready. When it came time for him to fly back to India for the crusade, the Lord told him not to get on the plane. He couldn't understand why not and reminded the Lord of the large amount of money and time already invested in the crusade. After arguing with the Lord for a while, he ended up not getting on the plane. A few days later, the horrible tsunami that took so many lives hit right in the exact area he was supposed to have held the crusade.

This man ended up making the right choice, the mature choice, but said that it was a very close decision because of the time and money already invested. I have thought about his situation more than once and wondered if I would have gotten on that plane. It is often our limited knowledge or natural type thinking that keeps us from understanding, believing, or acting on a message from the Lord. Proverbs 3:5 says it best, *"Trust in the lord with all your heart and lean not on your own understanding"* (NIV). When we truly do this, God can protect us from all of the "thorns" that are trying to choke us and make us unfruitful and immature.

PRODUCING A CROP

In this parable, we have seen that each of us are going to respond to the "words" or different messages that the Lord sends us in one of four ways. Jesus sums up the fourth response type in Matthew 13:23 *"...the seed that fell on good soil is the man who hears the word and understands it. He produces a crop, yielding a hundred, sixty, or thirty times what was sown"* (NIV). The proof that we have heard and understood a message from the Lord is that we accept it, retain it, and persevere until there is a crop. The crop or fruit validates this last choice.

There is a multiplication factor that exists when we are truly in the flow of what God is doing. As He multiplied the fish and loaves, He multiplies the effects of our meager efforts when we are obedient to Him and abiding in Him. As I heard someone say, He adds the super to our natural to get "supernatural" results. As He sows His seed in our hearts, and it comes to fruition, many, many, people will be touched. It becomes a chain reaction, whereby He compounds His efforts and effects through us. This is the fruit.

The great thing about this is that as long as we are alive, it is never too late to get on board with what God is doing. In the parable about the two sons, we might be like the first son who initially tells his Father "No," but ends up being obedient (see Matt. 21:28-32). This could be in regards to God in general or it could be just about a particular message or "word" that He has spoken to us. Our God is a God who restores the years eaten by the locusts when we rend our hearts and return to Him (see Joel 2).

The Lord literally called my name in a church when I was 19 to call me into ministry, but I ran from Him. After twenty years of alcohol and drugs and many bad choices, He stepped into my life and got me on a path back to Him. Shortly after that, a huge logging truck fell on top of me and basically severed my body in half. I had an out-of-body experience where I got to see the two angels that the Lord sent to save me. (Doctors say that I am the only person in the world known to have lived after having main arteries severed in my chest in five places.) During my year in and out of the hospital, and after five major operations, a documented creative miracle happened. The Lord gave me back several feet of small intestine so that I wouldn't end up starving to death, as most of my small intestine had been removed because of the accident.

After all of this, I ended up going into full-time, traveling ministry. I tell people what the Lord has done for me and for others and, more importantly, what He will do for them. We invite people forward for prayer and then get to sit back and watch God do amazing things. The Lord has shown me over and over that He wants to empower *all* believers to make an impact in this world, to produce fruit for His Kingdom. At times, the Lord will have me pray for people and, after some miracles have happened, the Lord tells me to have those people pray for the next people who pray for the next people and so on. Each time this has happened it has been very powerful, but one time stands out because the Lord Jesus appeared to explain what was happening.

I preached in a small, denominational church that I had been told was pretty dead. After speaking, I prayed for some people, at which point the Lord instructed me to tell the last person healed that they were to pray for the next in line and so on. As the miracles continued, the people in attendance were getting more and more excited and began to crowd around the altar and loudly praise God.

I stepped back from the group when the Holy Spirit instructed me to go over to a small area that housed the piano and to go inside. As I stepped into the area, I saw Jesus sitting at a pew that had been placed between the wall and the piano. His back was to the wall and He was looking out across the piano toward the people who were at the front of the church praying for each other and loudly praising Him. I instantly got down on my knees and placed my forehead on the carpet when He said, "No, come sit next to me."

I sat down next to Him and He pointed toward the people and said, "Do you see that? They don't even realize you're gone." As I contemplated the implications of that statement, He told me that it made Him happy and was exactly what He wanted: everyday people praying for each other and giving *God* all the glory. He ended by saying that I was to continue doing this same thing: to go into places and start fires in people's hearts for God and go to the next place and do the same thing.

Every Christian who has ever read the "Great Commission" has been given the same instructions from Jesus. We are all called into full-time ministry. It might not be your vocation, but as a Christian it should be your lifestyle. In Matthew's description, Jesus tells us to make disciples, baptize them, and teach them (see Matt. 28:18-20). In Mark's account of the Great Commission, Jesus says that "those who believe" will do many things including casting out demons and laying hands on sick people and watching them recover (see Mark 16:15-18). When the Lord speaks to us, we need to Hear Him, understand Him, and obey in order to produce a crop.

James 1:22 says, *"Do not merely listen to the word, and so deceive yourselves. Do what it says"* (NIV).

MORE ABOUT
AUTHOR BRUCE VAN NATTA

BRUCE VAN NATTA has been sent on a mission from Jesus to start fires in people's hearts for God. Since being crushed under a semi-truck and having an out-of-body experience where he witnessed the angels the Lord sent, he has gone into full-time ministry. Bruce founded Sweet Bread Ministries and now shares his gripping testimony worldwide and has been featured in several media outlets including the *700 Club*, Sid Roth, TBN, *Charisma* magazine, and *Guideposts*. He also authored the book *Saved By Angels* to share how God talks to everyday people. You can invite Bruce to speak at your church, conference, special event, or invite him to hold a workshop or seminar. Many people report being healed of all kinds of sicknesses, diseases, addictions, and emotional issues after attending one of Bruce's meetings. For more information visit sweetbreadministries.com or call 715-213-6116.

9

BECOMING A VOICE OF GOD

By Wilmer Singleton

The voice of the LORD is over the waters; the God of glory thunders; the LORD is over many waters. The voice of the LORD is powerful; the voice of the LORD is full of majesty. The voice of the LORD breaks the cedars, yes, the LORD splinters the cedars of Lebanon. He makes them also skip like a calf, Lebanon and Sirion like a young wild ox. The voice of the LORD divides the flames of fire. The voice of the LORD shakes the wilderness; the LORD shakes the Wilderness of Kadesh. The voice of the LORD makes the deer give birth, and strips the forests bare; and in His temple everyone says, "Glory!" (Psalm 29:3-9 NKJV)

Is there a voice of God in the earth today? Absolutely!

Every single person on the earth, whether a Believer or unbeliever, needs to hear the voice of God. There is not a single person who hasn't, at some point, needed wisdom in a certain situation—the type of wisdom that goes beyond experience or knowledge. The difference between a believer and an unbeliever is that the believer knows what is needed and should know where to find it. The power of the "still, small voice" can turn a hopeless situation into an "and-suddenly" experience. The power of the still small voice can expose the plans of the enemy and set you free from his schemes. The power of the still small voice can put you in the middle of the will of God for your life. Without the voice of God, you will never fulfill your destiny and God-given purpose for your life. Not only that, if you don't fulfill your destiny, countless others will not fulfill theirs. I propose to you that the destiny of nations is in the hands of the believer.

All believers want to hear and understand the voice of God and for various reasons. Some need deliverance, some want ministry, and some want to give glory to God. This chapter is for those who have a pure heart and desire to see the voice of God change nations and people, and not just to build prophetic ministries. Fulfilling a Kingdom mandate must point to Christ and His Kingdom and not to us. Too many people are building and advancing their own kingdoms and not the Kingdom of our God and Father. I believe that we are coming to a time when the pure voice of God will be heard and proved by the power it produces. We'll see those who have built their own kingdoms begin to fade, and we'll see their prayers hitting nothing but open air. When Jesus prayed, He hit the mark and that situation was changed. Our prayers *must* have the same purpose and power. We can't say, "Well, that was Jesus." That excuse does not fly, especially since we are made in the same image.

IN HIS LIKENESS

Then God said, "Let Us make man in Our image, according to Our likeness; and let them rule over the fish of the sea and over the birds of the sky and over the cattle and over all the earth, and over every creeping thing that creeps on the earth."

God created man in His own image, in the image of God He created him; male and female He created them (Genesis 1:26-27 NASB).

Jesus said in John 14:9, *"He who has seen Me has seen the Father"* (NASB). I believe that when people see us, they should see Jesus and ultimately the Father. They should see Him through us by the way we go about executing the judgments of God—not against people, but against the principalities and powers in high places. Our words execute judgment against cancers and disease, lack, and negative self-images. Our words even cancel appointments with death. God's will be done on earth as it is in Heaven. Remember, God created the heavens and the earth; therefore, God is not in Heaven, but rather, Heaven is in God. What that means is that Heaven didn't produce God, God produced Heaven. From His bosom came a dwelling place.

God's bosom can only produce and create perfection. That is exactly how He has always seen you and me. He had to, because, again, He saw us in His own image. Whenever we see something in someone's life that doesn't line up with the perfect will of God, we have authority to deliver the captive from the lies of the devil. We don't have authority over that person, but we do have authority over any spirit keeping that person from becoming the perfect will of God. Sickness and disease are under our feet. All addictions are under our feet, and it's our job to keep them there. God knew that these things would come; that's why He has always had a plan for us to have authority over all of these things and circumstances. These things are under the authority of the voice of God. God gives life to that which is dead and calls into existence things which do not exist.

> *Now faith is the assurance of things hoped for, the conviction of things not seen. For by it the men of old gained approval. By faith we understand that the worlds were prepared by the word of God, so that what is seen was not made out of things which are visible* (Hebrews 11:1-3 NASB).

True and accurate faith is founded on the Word of God. When that faith is in you it speaks, and when it speaks it is powerful. It has the same level of power as if God speaks it. The truth of the matter is that when you speak Holy-Spirit-filled words, He is speaking. God's Word should always come with a demonstration of power. Something changes in the spirit realm, so we must learn how to build in the Spirit in order to see change in the natural.

BECOMING ACCURATE BUILDERS IN THE SPIRIT

Becoming accurate builders in the Spirit is quite simply, praying accurate prayers—not just in words, but in Spirit and truth. Praying in Spirit and in truth are the necessary ingredients to producing words of power (see John 4:24). Praying from your soul realm, backed with love and emotions, is not the same as praying in the Spirit. When you or I pray for healing for a family member, we can't let our emotions take us out of our Spirit and into a place of hope or fear of loss. We must pray from a place of God-given authority and not hope. As our spiritual stature increases, so does the revelation knowledge of what it means to walk by faith and not by sight. We walk in faith of what God has done and not an empty faith that sounds good. God has given us the same authority that He gave to Jesus. Therefore, anything we see has to come into the perfect order of God. We don't walk by sight; we walk in God-given authority. Our faith is in that truth, and that truth has the power to heal, create, and execute the will of God in the natural realm. Whatever we build in the Spirit will manifest in the natural.

Building in the Spirit is praying in the Spirit. That literally means to allow the Holy Spirit of God to pray through us.

> *And the Holy Spirit helps us in our weakness. For example, we don't know what God wants us to pray for. But the Holy Spirit prays for us with groanings that cannot be expressed in words. And the Father who knows all hearts knows what the Spirit is saying, for the Spirit pleads for us believers in harmony with God's own will. And we know that God causes everything to work together for the good of those who love God and are called according to His purpose for them* (Romans 8:26-28 NLT).

I once heard a saying that went like this: "Whenever my life is not filled with prayer, coincidences stop happening." I love that. Not that we believe in coincidences, but when we are living prayer-filled lives things just seem to line up and divine protection is evident. This is the importance of praying in tongues. I have heard people say, "Tongues is not a Heaven or hell issue." That statement is incomplete and said from lips that are deceived. It may not be a Heaven or hell issue for a believer, but I have seen praying in tongues deliver lost souls from hell. As I said earlier in this chapter, we don't have authority over any person or the will of that person, but we do have authority over the spirits manipulating that person. Consistently praying in the Spirit concerning an individual will lead to his or her freedom. It's not a prayer that sounds like, "God will you save him?" He already saved all of us 2,000 years ago. It is authority that says to that lying spirit, *Go in Jesus' name!* Now if people love their sin, they will stay in it. You can deliver them and they go right back to bondage. But just because someone goes back does not speak to our authority or the power of our prayer lives.

Another Scripture I want to talk about is Ephesians 3:20 which says:

> *Now to Him who is able to do far more abundantly beyond all that we ask or think, according to the power that works within us.*

The power that works within us is the Holy Spirit; the evidence that He is working in us is praying in tongues. Praying in tongues is praying above what you can ask or think. God is a God of abundance. Not for the sake of flash, but for the purpose of us showing who He is to a dying world. The voice of God gives life. The earth is not bound for hell, it's bound for destiny in Christ. To accomplish this, it will take supernatural faith. Not normal, cute faith that hits the mark here and there, but most holy faith that will strip the cedars of Lebanon. How do we develop that kind of faith? By praying in tongues.

But you, beloved, building yourselves up on your most holy faith, praying in the Holy Spirit (Jude 20 NASB).

Can you image if our prayer actually brought Heaven to earth. What if we could pray from our seat in Heaven with creative power that casts down sickness, brings deliverance, and even brings rain to drought-stricken areas? Whatever you can imagine, He can do. He can abundantly do that and more. Our prophetic nature and power exposes the plans of the devil and brings the earth into alignment with the plans of God. God's plans trump anything the devil can come up with. He is looking for those who would stand up and release the voice of God into action. It better be you. You take your house and city for Jesus; be an accurate expression of Him who sent you and equipped you. It is God's desire that what is established in Heaven would be established here on earth. Is there sickness in Heaven? Are there diseases in Heaven? Is there lack in Heaven? He has given us the power to calm the raging storms, not just in our personal lives but also in the lives of those around us. We must bring Heaven to earth!

Pray, then, in this way: "Our Father who is in heaven, Hallowed be Your name. Your kingdom

come Your will be done, on earth as it is in heaven"
(Matthew 6:9-10 NASB).

Please don't tell me you think this is a cute Scripture that we can say but never see come to pass. There is a company of believers who will walk in this dimension of the Spirit. Become a part of it. Don't sit on the sideline—the sideline is for spectators and those who don't know the technology to bring home the victory. Look around at the people in your life and tell me they don't need some victory. But who can give it to them. I am telling you that it's you. Take what you receive and totally change your sphere of influence. Even those who are connected to you will see a change in their lives. The more Heaven is revealed in you, the more hell has to flee from around you. The gates of hell will not prevail. That doesn't sound like a defeated "waitin' on Jesus" apathetic movement to me. What are we waiting on Jesus for? He has already given us everything we need to advance His Kingdom. The Wise Master Builder isn't going to send us out to a job without equipping us to do the job He has called us to. God has blessed us with every spiritual blessing (see Eph. 1:3); so why are we seeking blessings when we are already blessed? As we walk in His will and purpose, the truth of who we are will manifest and we'll see lives changed for the glory of our Father.

The more and more we accurately pray in tongues, the more our lives will be in His perfect will. I'm not talking about empty tongue talking with no earth-changing power. We're not talking about shooting a machine gun and not knowing where the target is. But rather, I'm talking about accurate prayers that hit the mark every time. A renewed mind thinks on the things of God and knows His thoughts and intents. God is not trying to keep secrets *from* us; they are secrets *for* us. His desire is to reveal mysteries of Heaven. Praying in the Spirit does that every time. Have you had a dream that you could not find an interpretation for? Pray in tongues concerning it and the Holy Spirit will reveal it to you. The Holy Spirit knows every secret in the earth, under the earth, and above the earth. The Spirit is willing, but the flesh is weak. He is always willing and able to reveal mysteries. Let's tap into that power and find out exactly what Heaven is saying in every area of life. Again, I can't stress this enough, not just for our individual lives but also for those around us.

THE POWER OF BUILDING WITH A RENEWED MIND

A renewed mind is essential when talking about becoming the voice of God. The things of God are foolishness to a mind that has not been renewed. The carnal mind can't comprehend victory, only defeat. The carnal mind thinks for itself and has to be able to "figure it out." If the carnal mind can't see how something will benefit it, it wants nothing to do with it. A carnal mind is a mind that is conformed to this world.

> *Therefore I urge you, brethren, by the mercies of God, to present your bodies a living and holy sacrifice, acceptable to God, which is your spiritual service of worship. And do not be conformed to this world, but be transformed by the renewing of your mind, so that you may prove what the will of God is, that which is good and acceptable and perfect* (Romans 12:1-2 NASB).

Have you ever wondered what the will of God is for your life? Of course, we all have. One thing is for sure. The will of God for our lives is good, it's perfect, and it is acceptable to us. If there are things in your life that aren't good and perfect, you have the authority to be a voice of God and remove it. If there are things in your life that are unacceptable to you, renew your mind and remove it. Your life in the Spirit realm (Heaven) is perfect, it's good and it is acceptable to you. Building in the spirit with a renewed mind will cause that perfect life to manifest before you. I'm not saying it's overnight, but with consistency you will see it change into exactly what God has for you.

> *So this I say, and affirm together with the Lord, that you walk no longer just as the Gentiles also walk, in the futility of their mind, being darkened in their understanding, excluded from the life of God because of the ignorance that is in them, because of the hardness of their heart; and they, having become callous, have given themselves over to sensuality for the practice of every kind of impurity with greediness. But you did not learn Christ in this way, if indeed you have heard Him and have been taught in Him, just as truth is in Jesus, that, in reference to your former manner of life, you lay aside the old self, which is being corrupted in accordance with the lusts of deceit, and that you be renewed in the spirit of your mind, and put on the new self, which in the likeness of God has been created in righteousness and holiness of the truth* (Ephesians 4:17-24 NASB).

Whenever we pray in the Spirit, we must focus our mind on the issue we're praying for. We can't try to pray in our closet for someone with cancer while thinking about some other issue of life. A mind that goes to and fro is not conducive to receiving from Heaven. It's not mind manipulation; it's making sure that our thoughts are lining up with the truth of God's word. Whatever He says is the truth. When we pray, we must focus on the truth of what He says. The fact is we may know someone with cancer. The truth is that by His stripes they were healed. As we pray we are literally building a bridge to the truth of their healing. Not just for healing, for whatever manifestation of Heaven is necessary.

We live in a fallen world, but the voice of God can pick it up again. You can pick it up; you can change the world with your words. Let there be light! You have authority and power: pray and do not doubt. Unbelief is found in a carnal mind. Be renewed in the spirit of your mind and you will believe God for the impossible. God is spirit and we have to communicate with him spirit-to-spirit. We are first and foremost spiritual beings. That is why we can pray spiritual prayers and expect angels to move on our behalf. Welcome to the secret place of the most high God.

THE TRUTH ABOUT ANGELS

The LORD has established His throne in the heavens, and His sovereignty rules over all. Bless the LORD, you His angels, mighty in strength, who perform His word, obeying the voice of His word! Bless the LORD, all you His hosts, You who serve Him, doing His will. Bless the LORD, all you works of His, in all places of His dominion; bless the LORD, O my soul! (Psalm 103:19-22 NASB)

"Angels get me this; get me that; I command you in the name of Jesus. I might fire these angels and get some other ones." Have you ever heard that nonsense preached? If so, run. I don't know how these people are still alive unless they have repented. If you want angels to move on your behalf, be a voice of God. Angels perform His Word and obey His voice. His voice is not soulish, nor does it seek to self-promote.

His voice causes angelic activity. We didn't create angels, and they are not ours to command. Hebrews 1 says that angels *"are ministering spirits sent..."* (1:14 NASB). Sent by who? God. Who has authority over them? God. The only reason we feel like we need to command angels is because our prayers are not breaking through. Praying in the power of the Spirit will cause all of Heaven to move on your behalf. Dwelling in the secret place of the Most High provides safe shelter with angelic presence.

> *For He will give His angels charge concerning you,*
> *to guard you in all your ways. They will bear you*
> *up in their hands, that you do not strike your foot*
> *against a stone* (Psalm 91:11-12 NASB).

My belief is that God is able to instruct His angels better than me or you. In my family, we have seen this Scripture come to pass many times, and I have never had to tell them what to do. We have "and suddenly" happen on a regular basis, and we have never had to command them. We thank God for them everyday, and for all of the provision that God has sent. Angels are an awesome creation. When you are in a service and angelic activity begins to break out, it is fun. We can respond to them and interact with them in ways that are appropriate. We enjoy them, because they bring times of refreshing, but we don't worship them. Too many times I have seen services go from worshiping God to worshiping angels. Remember, they saw what happened to a chief angel who decided he wanted to be worshiped and wanted to be seated on the throne of God. If we worship angels, it will cause them to remove themselves from our midst. If you ever see an angel receiving worship, it is not true and from God. Angels work with us, comfort us, and protect us just for starters. They are sent on assignments concerning us. The one to be worshiped is the One who sent them.

Let's briefly recap. If you want to see angels move on your behalf it's simple: Pray spiritual prayers. God does not respond to our flesh or our soul. He responds to our spirit-man. Our spirit-man walks in faith and authority. When God hears our spirit-man praying, He calls into action all of Heaven: "Your kingdom come your will be done, on earth as it is in Heaven" (see Matt. 6:10 NASB). Our spiritual words cause God to command angels to bring our words to pass. So if you have been commanding angels, you now know what it takes to see them move on your behalf. Watch and see the difference as you practice the power of becoming the voice of God.

UNDERSTANDING THE VOICE OF GOD

Understanding the voice of God has a lot more to do with our hearts than it does our minds. God's voice never brings confusion, doubt, or unbelief. An important thing to remember about the voice of God is that it brings faith, revelation, and change. We have all said "God gave me a revelation." Not that it's not true, but the question I always ask myself is, *What changed?* True revelation brings change. It will change the way we think, the way we pray, the way we eat, the way we...you fill in the blanks. Understanding the voice of God changes us from the inside out. It brings about permanent change. We all want to change the world, but first our lives must be changed. When we walk with understanding we will walk with power. The more understanding we have, the more power and wisdom we will have as well. Let me put it this way, true understanding shows us how to use the wisdom we receive from hearing His voice. Understanding is vital to fulfilling what the Lord says.

> *The beginning of Wisdom is: get Wisdom (skillful and godly Wisdom)! [For skillful and godly Wisdom is the principal thing.] And with all you have gotten, get understanding (discernment, comprehension, and interpretation)* (Proverbs 4:7).

OVERCOMING THE UNFRUITFUL MIND

An unfruitful or carnal mind is the number one hindrance to hearing and understanding the voice of God. A carnal mind produces unbelief and fear and relies on worldly wisdom. It points back to self and points out all of the reasons why what God speaks can't come to pass. A renewed mind submits to the heart or spirit-man and allows itself to live by faith believing that with God all things are possible. The mind is designed to be an aid for us concerning the things of God, not a hindrance.

The focus of the carnal mind is the sin or war in the members. It focuses on the law, while a renewed mind thinks on the things of the spirit and sets its focus on forgiveness. A healthy renewed mind is able to receive the words of God because it believes more the power of God to bring it to pass than it does the sin or imperfections of the human life. The blood of Jesus has made us free from the law of sin and death. If we don't renew our minds, we will continually go back to bondage where our traditions make the word of God of no effect.

A renewed mind can see into the mind of the spirit. This gives us authority to build accurately in the Spirit. However, if your mind can't see it, your spirit can't build it. Once we are like-minded with the Holy Spirit, we are able to pray spiritual prayers and see the things we're focused on come to pass. Please hear me; we pray based on what the Spirit shows us, not what we show Him. We don't pray based on our emotions or what we want, or try to use mind power to bring things to pass. We are not New Agers. Remember, our minds submit to the spirit-man and the Holy Spirit. This allows for true eternal power that will set captives free and literally change the earth and the fullness thereof.

Our minds are not designed to figure God out. This is where we all fall short from time to time. We want to be able to conceive in our minds the things of God before we act on what He is speaking. This can be dangerous when prophesying because we try to explain how the prophecy will come to pass or we're trying to bring spiritual words down to a fleshly level. Or in the midst of prophesying we have a thought that says "I can't see how that can happen." You can't think those things and prophesy to the nations. If you don't believe that God can do anything, you have no business prophesying because when He speaks, He speaks based on what He knows of Himself and not what we believe or don't believe. This is why I believe the last thing that should be taught about prophecy is prophesying. Character and integrity lead the way along with a healthy and renewed mind. Unfortunately, prophecy is big business. If you can prophesy, you can have a ministry. Many prophesy and don't even know the One who gave the gift. There are many workers of iniquity who are seeking for themselves and not for the advancement of the Kingdom of God. Hearing and understanding the voice of God is not about your ministry, it's about you connecting with your Father and *re-presenting* Him to a dying world. Can these dry bones live? Absolutely!

And when I came to you, brethren, I did not come with superiority of speech or of wisdom, proclaiming to you the testimony of God. For I determined to know nothing among you except Jesus Christ, and Him crucified. I was with you in weakness and in fear and in much trembling, and my message and my preaching were not in persuasive words of wisdom, but in demonstration of the Spirit and of power, so that your faith would not rest on the wisdom of men, but on the power of God. Yet we do speak wisdom among those who are mature; a wisdom, however, not of this age nor of the rulers of this age, who are passing away; but we speak God's wisdom in a mystery, the hidden wisdom which God predestined before the ages to our glory; the wisdom which none of the rulers of this age has understood; for if they had understood it they would not have crucified the Lord of glory;

but just as it is written, "Things which eye has not seen and ear has not heard, and which have not entered the heart of man, all that God has prepared for those who love Him." For to us God revealed them through the Spirit; for the Spirit searches all things, even the depths of God. For who among men knows the thoughts of a man except the spirit of the man which is in him? Even so the thoughts of God no one knows except the Spirit of God. Now we have received, not the spirit of the world, but the Spirit who is from God, so that we may know the things freely given to us by God, which things we also speak, not in words taught by human wisdom, but in those taught by the Spirit, combining spiritual thoughts with spiritual words. But a natural man does not accept the things of the Spirit of God, for they are foolishness to him; and he cannot understand them, because they are spiritually appraised. But he who is spiritual appraises all things, yet he himself is appraised by no one. For who has known the mind of the lord, that he will instruct Him? But we have the mind of Christ (1 Corinthians 2 NASB).

I pray that everything that you read in this book will change your life. Not for the sake of ministry, but rather for the sake of knowing Him.

MORE ABOUT
AUTHOR WILMER SINGLETON

WILMER SINGLETON and his wife Rebecca are the founders of Freedom and Power Ministries. Wilmer is known for prophetic accuracy and a passion for healing the sick. He is a graduate of Jonathan David's Permanent School of the Prophets, known as one of the most relevant prophetic schools in the world. Wilmer teaches his own School of the Spirit and ministers life changing prayers on a regular basis. He is zealous about his family and advancing the Kingdom of God. He lives in South Central Pennsylvania with Beckie and their three boys Miciah, Elijah, and Josiah.

Conclusion

HEARING GOD'S VOICE

By Todd Hunter

You have just read some amazing stories. The stories pointed to ideas and concepts the various authors sought to communicate. Of course I cannot assume for sure how you reacted to the stories and teachings, but I think I can know one thing: You probably reacted based on your history and church background. This is of course true for the authors of this book—including me—the *summarizer*. None of us can stand apart from our past and our context. But that does not mean we cannot grow, change, and take on new practices.

My understanding of hearing God is, of course, also shaped by my experiences.

This being the case, you should know my background. It forms my thinking. It creates my biases for better or worse.

I first learned to hear the voice of God as a new convert at Calvary Chapel in the Southern California *Jesus Movement* of the 1970s. I heard God's voice loud and clear many times during Bible studies. I sensed God's voice in concerts or times of worshipful singing. We had special meetings in which people prophesied and gave words of knowledge and wisdom. I witnessed people, following what they thought were promptings from God, praying for others with great effect, sometimes including healings, but almost always blessing of some sort was reported. Why else would thousands of people keep coming back for more?

Later, in the Vineyard movement, I participated in these activities with an even greater emphasis. We were taught to hear from God and given the space to learn God's voice. We were encouraged that there was no *risk free* way to learn the difference between our own thoughts and the guidance, leading, and voice of God. We created safe places to experiment with hearing God's voice without turning the rest of the body of Christ into lab rats or guinea pigs. We had a value system in place that undergirded all of this: no hype, no exaggeration, no manipulation, honest reporting, humility, gentleness, and more.

We also had some agreed upon practices that kept things relationally and ethically safe and secure in the midst of great risk taking. No matter what happened in a given exchange we wanted the person being prayed for to walk away feeling loved, cared for, and supported—never chastised for lack of faith, etc. Recognizing the intimacy of ministry settings, we usually asked for permission to give words or lay our hands on people. In short, we sought to make relationally safe places in which to encounter our sometimes-dramatic God.

Over the last couple of decades, while holding onto earlier lessons and values, I have been learning about hearing the voice of God through the practices associated with spiritual formation. God's voice is surely heard in silence and solitude. He is heard in conversational prayer and meditation on Scripture. He is heard in the context of spiritual direction and liturgical forms of prayer.

I believe that hearing God is not meant to be only for special people—whatever that might mean in a given setting. Rather, hearing God is a normal aspect of an overall life in God, which is marked by conversation, by talking over with God the events of our lives—work, play, and "ministry." I practice everything I have learned from thirty years of mentors and teachers, those who have modeled for me ethical and effective ways of hearing God for the sake of others.

Do you struggle with this? Do some of the stories in this book seem out of reach for you? If so, you are not alone. Praying seems normal. But try telling your mother or cubicle-mate that God is speaking to you. Funny looks are apt to come your way. But, we must all face this reality: Almost every page of the Bible contains or is in some way animated by conversation between God and people.

If we accept this basic premise, we have a choice to make among several options:

> We can assume that God has changed since biblical times and that He no longer speaks.

> We can conclude that the people in the Bible were different than us, that they were somehow specially favored to hear from God.

> Or…

> God is still speaking to ordinary people and we just need to incline our ears to Him and find

faith-filled, risk-taking, but humble ways to hear Him. And when called to do so, report what we hear in service to others.

Obviously, the writers of this book and I commend the latter. But please know this: You do not have to hear God or talk about hearing God in the ways the authors do. You can have a conversational relationship with God that fits your personality, your temperament, and your gift mix. You can do so in ways that are fit for your church and your community. You can learn to hear and express what you hear in ways that others around you experience it as for their good.

There is no need to mimic others, no need for religious pretension or over-confident posturing. In fact, you will be most ethical and effective when you ground yourself in humility and tentativeness. Even after three decades of learning to hear from God, I still say to people: "I may be wrong, but I think God might be saying...."

Such an unassuming nature is crucial. It keeps things real—I am very fallible. It keeps the one hearing the word in charge of his or her life before God. It gives God space to work directly with the receiving person, thus leaving that person with the notion that God knows them, looks after them, and loves them.

On the other hand, if we suck all the oxygen from the room in an effort to promote ourselves, the Spirit is grieved and the receiving person is left confused or in adulation of us.

In the introduction, we told you what we were going to tell you. The various authors then told you. Now I've just *told* you again. There is now just one thing left—get started. Hearing God and sharing it with others is better caught than taught. It is a practiced reality, not a conceptual or abstract one. You only learn by doing.

Hearing God: keep it real...keep it simple...keep it humble... and keep it going for the sake of serving others.

ABOUT FRANK DECENSO, JR.

Frank DeCenso is the author of *Presence Powered Living: Building a Life of Intimacy and Partnership with God*, published by Vineyard International Publishers. His website is http://presencepowered.com. He lives in Virginia Beach, Virginia, with his wife of 15 years.

More Information About the Authors

Dr. Jane Hamon
pjhamon@yahoo.com

Christy Wimber
Yorbalindavineyard.com

Dr. Barbie Breathitt
barbiebreathitt@sbcglobal.net

Dr. Scott McDermott
www.crossingumc.org

Jason Westerfield
www.kingdomreality.com

Katie Souza
www.expectedendministries.com

Kevin Dedmon
kevindedmon.com

Rob Coscia
www.diamondvc.org

Bruce Van Natta
vannatta@wctc.net

Wilmer Singleton
www.destinyprayer.com
info@destinyprayer.com

In the Right Hands, This Book will Change Lives!

Most of the people who need this message will not be looking for this book. To change their lives, you need to put a copy of this book in their hands.

> *But others (seeds) fell into good ground, and brought forth fruit, some a hundred-fold, some sixty-fold, some thirty-fold* (Matthew 13:8).

Our ministry is constantly seeking methods to find the good ground, the people who need this anointed message to change their lives. Will you help us reach these people?

> *Remember this—a farmer who plants only a few seeds will get a small crop. But the one who plants generously will get a generous crop* (2 Corinthians 9:6).

**EXTEND THIS MINISTRY BY SOWING
3 BOOKS, 5 BOOKS, 10 BOOKS, OR MORE TODAY,
AND BECOME A LIFE CHANGER!**

Thank you,

Don Nori Sr., Founder
Destiny Image
Since 1982

DESTINY IMAGE PUBLISHERS, INC.

*"Speaking to the Purposes of God for This Generation
and for the Generations to Come."*

VISIT OUR NEW SITE HOME AT
WWW.DESTINYIMAGE.COM

FREE SUBSCRIPTION TO DI NEWSLETTER

Receive free unpublished articles by top DI authors, exclusive

discounts, and free downloads from our best and newest books.

Visit www.destinyimage.com to subscribe.

Write to: Destiny Image
              P.O. Box 310
              Shippensburg, PA 17257-0310

Call: 1-800-722-6774

Email: orders@destinyimage.com

For a complete list of our titles or to place an order
online, visit www.destinyimage.com.